Step by Step

Adventures in Sequencing with Max/MSP

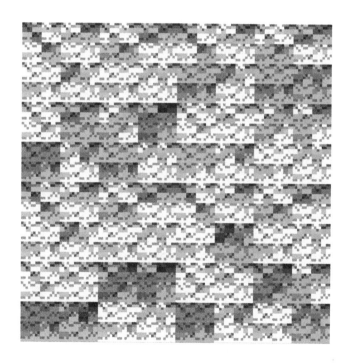

Gregory Taylor

Step by Step: Adventures in Sequencing with Max/MSP by Gregory Taylor

Published by
Cycling `74
340 S. Lemon Avenue #4074
Walnut, CA 91789 USA
www.cycling74.com

First edition

Design and formatting by Ivan Kamaldinov
Typeset in Apercu Pro
Cover by Gregory Taylor

Kindle ISBN: 978-1-7325903-0-4

For Darwin and my friends at Cycling '74

— mentors, interlocutors, enablers, and refiners of my "good ideas"

Introduction   8

How This Book Works   11

First Steps — A Simple Step Sequencer   15

My First Step Sequencer   17
The Joys of Abstraction   18
Stopping and Starting   24
Setting Things Up   32
To Play Or Not To Play   35
Taking a List and Making Some Noise   40
The Joys of Being a Joiner   41
Listening To The Sequencer   43
Working With Softsynths   45
Working with VST/AU Synths   46
Working With AMXD devices (for Max Users)   49

Building Out – Count On It   51

One Is The Loneliest Number   53
On A Roll   58
Rinse and Repeat   61
Know When To Fold `em   63
A Final Word   65

Step By Step – live.step, Part 1   68

Keeping it Simple   70
Polyphony?   74
A Little Animation   81
Food For Thought   83

To Play Or Not To Play, Part 1   84

Heads Or Tails?   87
What's the Chance of That Happening?   92
Location Location Location   98
Playing The Odds   101

Questions of Scale(s): Transposition and Mapping   105

Note Filtering   109
Scales and Modes   115
Arbitrary Scale Mapping   121

Step By Step – live.step, Part 2   127

Forging The Chain   129
Keeping Things Odd   133
Right On Time   136

Beating Time   146

Dividing Your Time: phasor~ and rate~   149
N-tuplets   154
Polyrhythms   157

To Play Or Not To Play, Part 2   161

Event Density (the drunkard's walk)   163
Location Location Location (Once Again)   169
To Play Or Not To Play (Euclidean version)   171
Dealing With Distribution   175
Location Location Location (One More Time)   180
Heavy Rotation   184

Step By Step – live.step, Part 3   190

Sequence to Dictionary – Fill 'er Up   193
Using The Dictionary   201
From Many Queries, One   202

Learning To Swing   208

Playing Early (and often)   213
Every bang for Itself   219
Another Source of Enlightenment   223

The Next Step(s)   224

Thinking Beyond the Note   226
Numbers As Voltages   229
Numbers As Parameters – VST/Audio Unit Plug-ins   233
Numbers As Parameters – AMXD Devices   242
Numbers As Parameters – The Live Object Model   253

Afterwords   262

Big Ideas and Little Steps   264
Recombining and Making Hybrids   265
The Zen of All Max Patching (The Three Questions)   266
Recycling Your Best Ideas   268
And Finally, a Few Words of Thanks and Praise...   270

Introduction

You never forget your first step sequencer.

Mine was an original Korg SQ-10 that I bought for a song from a guy who was trying to get rid of an old MS-20. On the way out the door, I noticed the SQ-10 over in the corner and tacked a little more money onto my offer on a whim. It came home with me, and I used it all the time. I've still got it and have many pleasant memories of teaching it new patching tricks (such as connecting the click track out on my old Electro-Harmonix 16-second delay line to the trigger input of the SQ-10 and then running the output through the delay as it galloped along).

With the arrival of Max and – in its time – MSP, I realized that I finally had the tools to "do it right" – to build *my sequencer*. I figured that trying to create the Next Big Thing in step sequencers would be a great encouragement when it came to learning Max – I'd have a reason and a goal. But along the way, I discovered something important: *There was no Next Big Thing*.

Let me explain.

Korg SQ-10

~~Next~~　　~~Big~~　　~~Thing~~

There's wasn't a Next.

There's wasn't a Big.

Finally, there wasn't a Thing.

My progress wasn't – and still isn't – linear. Bits and pieces of what I once considered to be my major project have disappeared and reappeared, morphed, and were reused and changed into other things entirely in a way that had nothing to do with the kind of progress associated with the word "next."

Rather than making a single huge patch that "did everything," I found myself making smaller and more specialized patches for specific purposes.

That is, the future is plural. My sequencer patch based on the SQ-10 is still around, along with a dozen descendants and distant relations. And, when someone posts video from the most recent Eurorack show that has some intriguing wrinkle, it's back to the drawing board.

So here I am, starting a series of tutorials for beginning users on the subject of... the step sequencer.

How This Book Works

The patches created and used in Step By Step don't comprise a regular tutorial in the sense that we're going to build a single finished ultra-deluxe Max patch. Instead, we are going to start with a simple step sequencer patch and then do something that Max programmers do all the time: *build out* from that basic patch in ways that add new features, showing ways to modify what's already there, and discussing how those changes affect the final product.

Building out from the original patch doesn't necessarily involve making a single complex change, either – rather, we'll show you several *different ways* that you can make changes in each of the individual parts of the simple step sequencer. One of my friend and colleague Tim Place's favorite characterizations of discovery is this:

Discovery consists of seeing what everybody has seen and thinking what nobody has thought.

I hope that the approach in this book allows you room to do just that.

It's really not the case that "the final example" in each chapter is the only interesting or the best variant – programming in Max is always about being unafraid of simple solutions: I think that one of the things that separates good Max programmers from great ones is a sensitivity to the point at which *"the perfect becomes the enemy of the good."*

As you learn Max, you may find someone else's examples confusing because you don't have a way to visualize the sequence of steps that led to the patch you're looking at – it helps to see the starting point and a sequence of addition and modifications. In addition, when you can't tell how or why things were added or changed, it's easy to imagine that a patch is made in one go by someone who was super smart, and to despair. The truth is that all those cool (and scary-looking) patches and devices are *themselves* a product of the technique of starting with something and then adding new features to it.

While this book doesn't assume you're a power user, it does assume that you've done some really basic work learning the essentials of Max:

- How to unlock a patch

- What Max messages are and what they do

- Opening, using, and patching from Max help files

- The basic structure of the MIDI messages we use to play notes using the MIDI standard

- Creating and using snapshots to save the state of a Max patch

These can all be found in the Basic Max tutorials and Max guides, and you might want to either look at them or refresh your knowledge before you start. I've tried to keep things simple, but I do expect you're familiar with some basic patching skills.

All of the Max patches created for this tutorial are available for you to upload from the following URL:

https://s3.amazonaws.com/cycling74-books/StepbyStep_Patches.zip

I hope that you'll read along and follow through these tutorials and develop a greater sense of confidence about patching. It's also my hope that you'll feel free to take parts of what's here and mix and match to make something of your own or create your own point of departure. May this book bring you joy and provide you with ways to bring more beauty into the world.

Gregory Taylor
gregory@cycling74.com

First Steps —
A Simple Step Sequencer

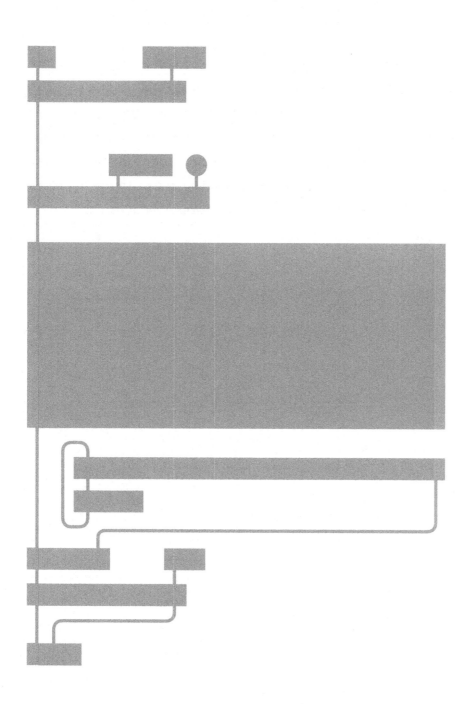

This isn't going to be a book whose goal is to to create a single finished ultra-deluxe Max patch. The starting point for patching in this book is a simple step sequencer patch that I'll walk you through in this chapter – I'll describe each of its basic component parts and show you how they fit together. The patch provides the point from which everything else follows – we'll be building out by adding new features and showing ways to modify what's already there, and discussing how those changes affect the final product. Those different ways of building out from the initial patch are possibilities you can combine to suit your own interests or needs. Let's get started!

My First Step Sequencer

The file *01_simple_step_sequencer* contains the step sequencer patch we're going to start with:

The patch contains a few basic components and several Max abstractions that do things for us as a part of the patch.

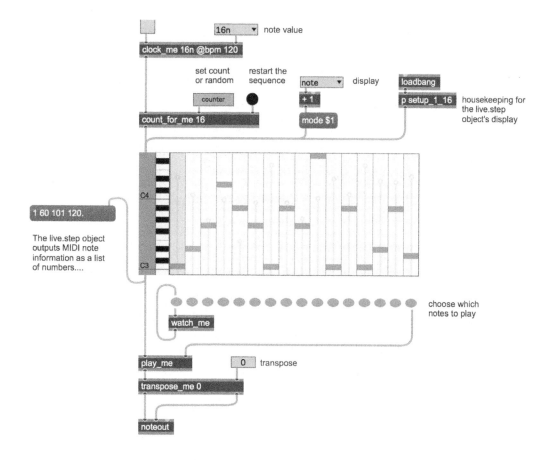

The Joys of Abstraction

The example Max patches in these tutorials all make use of *abstractions* – the ability to have parts of your patching logic live in separate, reusable files that you can then use inside of any Max patcher you like.

You'll notice that you have Max patches in the Chapter 1 tutorial patches folder that have the same names as objects in your example patch – *clock_me, play_me, count_for_me, watch_me, transpose_me*, and so on. They started out as standard Max patcher files. Each patcher object contained the same set of Max objects as the abstractions do. All we did was to save the contents of the patchers as separate files, and to put the saved the abstractions into the same folder as the example patches. To use any one of those abstractions, you just type its name into an empty Max object box and save your patch. When you launch the example patches, the abstractions will be loaded and ready to use.

In addition, you can modify abstractions so that they can use arguments and attributes to set initial values in the same way that regular Max objects do. This is done using the **patcherargs** object. We'll show you this technique in action later in this tutorial, and you'll see it used again and again throughout this book.

Note

One thing to be careful of as you use abstractions is that it is *never* a good idea to give an abstraction the same name as a Max external (naming an abstraction "delay," for instance). You'll notice that all of the abstractions I've created in each of the folders associated with chapters in the book have names that include underscore characters and occasional names that reference Alice in Wonderland such as play_me or transpose_me), and I have never given the same name to two different abstractions. That's also good Max patching practice.

For more on abstractions, see the Max Basic Tutorial 15: Abstractions

Here are the basic components of our simple step sequencer, in order:

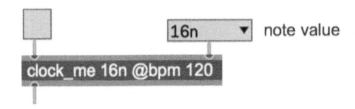

The **clock_me** abstraction at the very top functions as a clock. It sets the rate at which the step sequencer runs. The object specifies its output rate using musically intuitive Time Value Syntax values (*4n* refers to a quarter note, *4nd* to a dotted quarter note, and 4nt to a quarter note triplet, etc.)

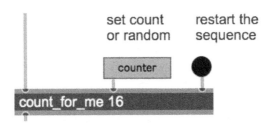

The Max **count_for_me** abstraction takes the output of the **clock_me** abstraction and produces either a count in the range of 1 – 16 or a random number in that same range that determines which note in our sequence we're going to output.

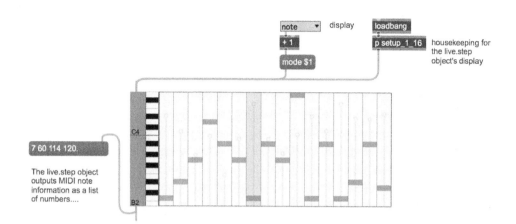

The **live.step** user interface object is the heart of the sequencer. It stores the MIDI note events for a sequence and lets you edit them graphically. It is one of those really useful Max objects that provides a lot of useful functionality the moment you add it to your patch, and helps us keep things simple.

With each step, the **live.step** object sends out a list of numbers we can use to play a MIDI note. The output list is composed of three integers and a floating-point number:

1. The number of the step in the sequence

2. A number that specifies the MIDI key we want to play

3. A number that specifies a velocity for the MIDI note event (which corresponds to how "hard" we hit the key)

4. The duration of the MIDI note event (i.e. how long we hold the key down)

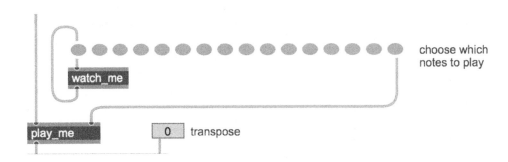

The Max **play_me** and **watch_me** abstractions control which MIDI note events in a sequence will be played to let you add variety to the output of our sequencer. There's one button for each step in the sequence. The **watch_me** abstraction notices when you click on a step, and tells the **play_me** abstraction to turn playback off or on by selectively sending the four-number MIDI note event list on to the next part of the patch. Old-school analog sequencer folks will recognize this skip feature right away!

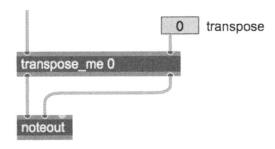

The **transpose_me** abstraction lets you transpose the pitch of the MIDI note event by adding or subtracting from its initial pitch value – adding a 1 transposes the sequence up a half-step, and subtracting 12 transposes the sequence down a full octave. The **transpose_me** abstraction also handles formatting a MIDI message to your software synth or external MIDI controller in the right order.

The **noteout** object sends MIDI note messages to an outboard MIDI device, or a softsynth hosted in Max (or in a Max for Live device). It's the end of the line.

As you can see, we've broken our step sequencer down into a series of component parts, each of which performs a specific task. Next, let's look at each of these component parts in more detail, to see how each part does its work.

Stopping and Starting

The **clock_me** abstraction provides the timekeeping for our step sequencer. You can turn it on and off using a **toggle**, set an overall tempo you want to use, and also set the rate at which is runs by selecting a note value from a **live.menu** object.

There's a little more going on inside the abstraction. Double-click on the **clock_me** abstraction to see its contents:

First, we've provided a simple way to "start" the abstraction that sends **bang** messages to the rest of our step sequencer from outside, and to set the tempo we want to use.

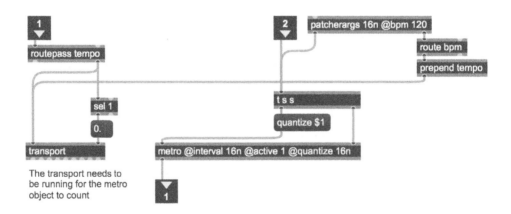

We've attached a **routepass tempo** object to the left inlet to do that. The **routepass** object takes a message as an argument (say, *tempo 120*), checks to see whether the first part of the message matches its arguments and – if so – sends the entire message (*tempo 120*) out the outlet that corresponds to the argument (this is similar to the Max **route** object, but the first item in the message isn't stripped off). This lets us set the tempo by sending the message *tempo <bpm value>* to the left inlet of the abstraction.

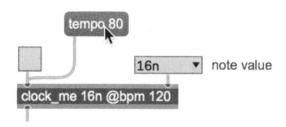

It also means that we can use the left inlet to handle input from the **live. toggle** object in the parent patch that turns things on and off – a 0/1 from the toggle gets passed out the **routepass** object's right outlet for a task I'll describe in just a minute.

Max has the convenient ability to let you use a central timekeeping object – a Max **transport** object. When you use a **transport** object in conjunction with a **metro** object, you can use metrical notation to set the **metro** object's rate. For example:

- *1n, 2n, 4n,* and *8n* refer to whole notes, half notes, quarter notes, and eighth notes, respectively

- *1nd, 2nd, 4nd,* and *8nd* refer to dotted versions of the note values

- *1nt, 2nt, 4nt,* and *8nt* refer to triplet versions of the note values

The **metro** object gets its information from the **transport** object for its current tempo, so you can modify the tempo and have your **metro** object automatically track the transport (instead of having to recalculate intervals in milliseconds, as the **metro** object usually does). If you're a Max for Live user, the Live application's transport broadcasts tempo information to your Max for Live device.

There are a few bits of housekeeping to take care of to make all this run smoothly, and we use attributes to the **metro** object to set them up.

1. We need to configure the **metro** object so that it runs when the **transport** object is on and broadcasting timing information. That's done by setting the *@active* attribute to a value of *1*.

2. We'd like to set an initial value for our **metro** object, and we'll set the **metro** object's *@interval* attribute to *16n* for that. Any time the **transport** object is turned on, the **metro** object will output *bang* messages at a rate corresponding to sixteenth notes at the current tempo.

3. Although using *@interval 16n* will cause the metro object to output *bang* messages at a rate that corresponds to the current tempo of the transport, the first *bang* message will not necessarily be synchronized with sixteenth notes in the transport object – the *bang* messages will merely be separated by an amount of time that corresponds to a sixteenth note. We need to have a way to synchronize that first *bang* message to be in time with the transport itself. Setting the *@quantize* attribute for the *metro* object to *1* will do just that.

4. Finally, we'll want to be sure that we set the *@quantize* attribute
   to match the timing setting for our **metro** object if we change the
   note value, so we'll add a **trigger** object **(t s s)** to send the note value
   received in the right inlet of the abstraction and also to pass that
   note value along to a **message** box to send the message *quantize
   <note value>* whenever it changes.

Everything's just about ready. But what about setting the tempo of the
clock_me abstraction? The basic step sequencer patch doesn't include
any message like *tempo 98* being sent to the abstraction. What's up with
that?

We could certainly open the Global Transport in Max by choosing it from
the **Extras** menu and typing a value into the tempo box:

But we really don't need to, because we've already set the tempo using
an attribute we set when we created the abstraction in our patch *(@bpm
120)*.

You might have noticed something interesting about the **count_for_me**
abstraction – it has arguments and attributes **(clock_me 16n @bpm 120)**
just like a regular Max object.

It can be useful to specify an initial state for a Max abstraction with arguments and @-*sign* attributes, just as we do with ordinary Max externals. In fact, you'll see that done in other abstractions in the simple step sequencer patch.

While we could just have used arguments inside of the patch for this specific use, it would be a lot nicer to be able to use the patch for any *other* range we might want to use for our sequencer at some future point. The **clock_me** abstraction includes a Max trick to do this by the inclusion of a **patcherargs** object. Let's look inside the abstraction one more time:

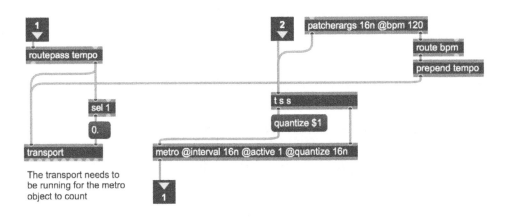

The **patcherargs** object in our abstraction itself takes an argument and an abstraction that should look familiar to you: one argument *(16n)* and one attribute *(@bpm 120)*. You'll notice that both the argument and the attribute involve specific values – those values set the default behavior of the abstraction that contains them.

The left outlet of the **patcherargs** object outputs any argument we type into the **clock_me** abstraction's object box (**clock_me 4n** or **clock_me 8n**, for example) and sends that value to the **trigger** object to set the interval and quantization for our **metro** object.

In turn, the right outlet of the **patcherargs** object outputs a message that contains the contents of any attribute names and values we type into the abstraction's object box (e.g. **clock_me @bpm 98** or **clock_me @bpm 240**). We use a **route** object to grab that value, pass the result through a **prepend tempo** object, and send the resulting tempo *<bpm>* message to the transport to set its tempo.

That's all there is to it. This technique can be very useful in your Max patching, and you'll be seeing the **patcherargs** object in use again and again throughout the chapters in this book.

Knowing When To Start Over –
The Counter

The **count_for_me** abstraction lets us either step through our sequence in order, randomly trigger any step, and also restart our count at 1. Selecting counter or random output is set by using a **live.text** object that we've configured to use as a toggle switch with text labels. Let's look inside the abstraction:

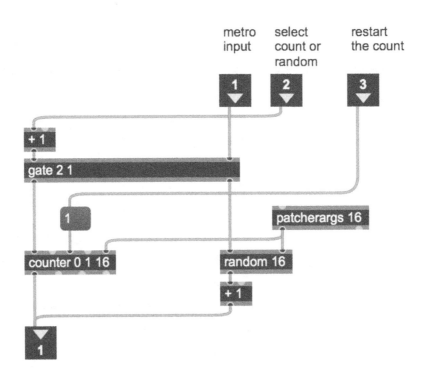

The **count_for_me** abstraction receives *bang* messages from the **clock_me** abstraction in the parent patch in its left inlet. A **gate** object is used to route those *bang* messages to one of two destinations selected according to input in the second inlet. That input comes from a **live.text** object in the parent patch, which we've set up to work like a button.

The **gate** object needs a value of 1 or 2 value to route the *bang* messages, and the **live.text** object is sending us a 0 or 1, so we'll need to add one to the input to control the **gate** object. We used arguments to specify the number of outputs from the **gate** object, and what the initial state of the gate should be — outputting *bang* messages to the **counter** object (**gate 2 1**). If we select random output by clicking on the **live.text** object in the parent patch, then the *bang* message will be sent to a **random 16** object, which will give us a random number between 0 and 15. We add 1 to that, and we've got a random selection of steps in our sequencer!

The **counter** object is ready to go by virtue of having used arguments to set the direction of the count and its range (**counter 0 1 16**). The only other control that would be useful would be to have a way to reset our sequencer so that it goes back to the first step (just like my old hardware step sequencer!). A *bang* message in the right inlet of the abstraction is connected to a **message** box, which will send the *message 1* to the third inlet in the **counter** object. Doing that sets the step of the sequence to be played to the first note in the sequence the next time the counter receives a *bang* message from the **clock_me** abstraction.

Finally, we've added a Max **patcherargs 16** object and connected it to the second inlet of the random object (to set the range of **random** numbers used when randomly choosing a step for our sequencer) and the right outlet of the **counter** object (to set the upper limit for the count).

Setting Things Up

The **live.step** object is the center of our patch, and does nearly all of the heavy lifting: it contains a single sequence of data composed of sixteen steps. Each step stores MIDI note information for pitch, velocity, and duration – everything we need to play a MIDI note on a software synth or an external MIDI instrument. We can also edit the sequence by clicking and dragging. The **live.step** object contains two bits of patching that help to set up the look and behavior of the **live.step** object and also give us access to the portions of the sequence we might want to edit.

In its default state, the **live.step** object shows us a piano roll of MIDI notes that we can alter by clicking on new notes or dragging an existing note up or down. In order to be able to change the velocity or duration of a note event, we need a way to display that information and make it available for editing. That's done using the message mode *N*, where *N* corresponds to the part of the MIDI note message we want to edit:

- *mode 1* displays MIDI note numbers

- *mode 2* displays velocities

- *mode 3* displays time durations.

We use a *live.menu* object set up to display those three options, connect the *live.menu* object's left outlet to send the number of the menu option we've suggested, and then a + 1 object to give us a number in the range 1 – 3 (like many Max objects, the *live.menu* object counts from 0 rather than 1).

Max UI objects let you use messages to set how the object looks and behaves. In lots of cases, you only need to do this once – when you initially load the program.

Our simple sequencer patch includes a Max abstraction that will be triggered any time the patch is loaded (by a Max **loadbang** object) to do just that: the **setup_1_16** abstraction. Double-clicking on the patcher will show you what's inside: a single **message** box full of individual messages to the **live.step** object, separated by commas so that they're sent sequentially.

Here's what the individual messages do:

* *nseq 1* sets the number of sequences stored by the **live.step** object.

* *nstep 16* sets the number of MIDI note events stored in the sequence.

* *mode 0* displays MIDI note events when we start the patch (rather than velocity or duration data.

* *loopruler 0* hides a part of the **live.step** display we're not using.

- *usestepcolor2 0* sets all of the MIDI note events to be the same color.

- *pitch_active 1* sets the **live.step** object to store and display MIDI note number information.

- *velocity_active 1* sets the object to store and display MIDI velocity information.

- *duration_active 1* sets the object to store and display MIDI note duration information.

- *display_seq 1* sets the number of stored sequences to be displayed. Since we are working with only one sequence, the number is set to 1 (yes, the **live.step** object counts the number of sequences it stores (up to 16) starting at 1 rather than 0).

- *target_seq 1* sets the number of the sequence we want to graphically edit. Since we're working with only one sequence, the number is set to 1, as with the display_seq message.

There are a lot of other options for setting up this object. If you want to know more, you can check the **live.step** object's help file, or use the object's Reference page for a complete description of all the messages and attributes associated with it.

To Play Or Not To Play

The next section of our simple sequencer handles turning output from individual steps in the sequence on or off, using a Max **matrixctrl** object to provide a user interface for setting on/off states, and two additional patcher files to translate what you see and click on to the way the patch passes information.

The **matrixctrl** object provides a quick and easy way to create a grid of switches, and can be used in all kinds of situations – you'll see it used throughout the course of the chapters in this book. You can use the object's Inspector to set the number of columns and rows (in our case, one row that contains each of the 16 steps in the sequencer). Clicking in a locked patcher will change the settings on each cell in the sequence from a 1 to a 0 or vice-versa.

Sending the message getrow *N*, where *N* is the number of the row you want to see, will send a list of ones and zeros out the right outlet of the **matrixctrl** object (since the **matrixctrl** object counts from 0 we send the message *getrow 0*).

There's just one little problem: clicking on one of the 16 switches doesn't *automatically* send that list out the right outlet, so we'll need to add a little Max patching to do that for us. That's just what the **watch_me** abstraction does. It takes advantage of the fact that clicking on any of the 16 switches does send a 3-number list out the left outlet of the **matrixctrl** object – *<row> <column> <switch-state>* (so the first switch being turned off is *0 0 0*, for example). A little smart Max patching will let us make good use of that. Here's what's inside of the **watch_me** abstraction:

Any time we click on any button on the **matrixctrl** object, we send that list to the **zl change** object, which checks to see if anything has changed. If so, it sends a bang out the right outlet and sends the *getrow 0* message we need back to the **matrixctrl** object, which then outputs that nice 16-item list.

Now that we have a nice list of open or closed switches, we can take the list output from the **live.step** object and set whether the MIDI note messages will be sent for any step in the sequencer or not.

Double-click to open the **play_me** abstraction and look inside:

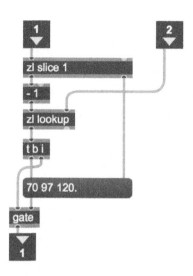

The **play_me** abstraction uses a technique for working with lists that you'll be seeing in use again and again throughout the rest of this book. It features two versions of a Max external object that functions as the all-purpose Swiss Army Knife for list processing — the **zl** object. The **zl** object is actually a whole family of list processing objects rolled into one: you choose the kind of list processing you want to do by providing arguments to the **zl** object that determine what it's going to do and how it's going to do it. There are two different versions of the **zl** object in this patch: **zl slice 1** and **zl lookup**. Here's how the patch works:

The patch has two inlets. The first inlet receives the list of four numbers (event number, note number, velocity and duration), and the second inlet contains a list of ones and zeros that corresponds to which notes we want to play or mute. The first **zl** object has two arguments: slice, which determines what the object will do to a list (i.e. it'll cut it into two pieces), and how much it will cut off of the list each time (in this case, the second argument says that we'll remove only one item). So, the **zl slice 1** object takes that list and divides it into two lists – a sliced-off list that contains the number of the event, and a second list that contains the MIDI note information. The MIDI note information is sent to the second inlet of a **message** box at the bottom of the patch, where it waits to be sent along if the note is played.

The second **zl**-family object in our abstraction – **zl lookup** – takes a list as input in its right inlet and then "looks up" and outputs the nth item in the stored list. There's a bit of a wrinkle, though – the **live.step** object numbers sequencer events starting from 1, while the **zl** family of objects number events from 0 (as most computers do). We can fix that easily by adding a **− 1** object, but it's something to keep in mind while you're patching
live.step output and processing those lists using **zl** objects.

The result from the list lookup is then sent to a **trigger (t)** object. The **trigger** object lets us take input and use it to sequence the order in which things are done later on in a patch. In this case, the trigger object does two things in a specific order, as set by the arguments to the object **(t b i)** – remember that objects send outputs from right to left.

1. It sends the 0/1 value to the first inlet of a **gate** object. If the value is a one, the **gate** object will send any input to its right inlet on, and a value of zero will prevent the **gate** object from sending anything through.

2. After the gate has been opened or closed, the **trigger** object sends a bang message to the **message** box that contains the three MIDI note information values we stripped off of the original input message, which will send those values to the **gate** object.

The great thing about using those **zl** objects in this patch means that we don't really care how long the list of on/off switches is; the abstraction will do its job no matter what. This kind of reusability is a good Max patching habit to develop.

Taking a List and Making Some Noise

Our simple sequencer has almost made it through the playing of a single note in our sequence – all we need to do is to assemble the three numbers in our list into a standard MIDI note message. The Max **makenote** object is made for just such a purpose – it's a perfect way to manage MIDI note output without having to manage note-off generation (You specify a duration for the note, and the **makenote** object does the rest for you). Our input list from the **play_me** abstraction consists of everything we need: a MIDI note number, a velocity value, and a duration value.

But there's just one more thing we can do here: we can take the MIDI note number and transpose our sequence on the fly by merely adding or subtracting from the first item in the list. The **transpose_me** abstraction does just that for us, and includes a Max object – one of a pair of objects, in fact – that may be new to you.

The Joys of Being a Joiner

If you've spent some quality time with the Max basic tutorials, you're probably used to using the Max **pack** and **unpack** object whenever you want to put together or take apart lists. In the course of this tutorial, I'm going to be using a pair of Max objects that you may be less familiar with: **join** and **unjoin**.

They're used for the same purpose, but have a few features that we thought you might find useful. First, you don't need to specify the data types in the list that you're packing or unpacking by typing something like **unpack i i f** – you just give the **join/unjoin** object an argument that specifies how many outlets you need (**unjoin 3**). I've gotten into the habit of using it because I'll often type the wrong data type as an argument or type in the wrong number of inlets and outlets. The **unjoin** object is just easier to type, too.

The **join** object works the same way as the **unjoin** object – it doesn't need to know what kinds of data you're going to send it – it just wants to know the number of inlets. For those of you who use the **pak** object to do the list packing regardless of which inlet receives new data, you can add an attribute with a special argument – *@triggers -1* – to transform a join object into the equivalent of a **pak** object.

The *transpose_me* abstraction contains our first example of these objects at work. Double-click on the abstraction to see what's inside:

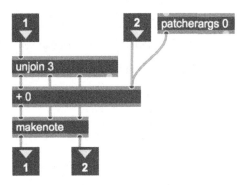

Inside the patcher, an **unjoin 3** object splits the note-velocity-duration list into individual messages and passes them along in order. We take the right and middle outputs of the **unjoin 3** object and send them directly to the **makenote** object, since transposing a note won't change either of those values. All we care about is the very first item in the list, which is output from the left outlet of the **unjoin** object.

Transposing our note is really simple: we have a second inlet to the patcher that receives the amount to add to or subtract from the initial MIDI note number. When that addition/subtraction is done, the new value is passed along to the **makenote** object. Since the **makenote** object's left inlet is the hot inlet (as is the case with nearly all Max objects), it outputs the sequence of MIDI note messages *only* when that left inlet receives a message.

A MIDI note is turned on and then turned off a specified amount of time later, and the resulting note and velocity information is sent out the patcher's outlets to the waiting **noteout** object in the parent patch.

Listening To The Sequencer

As you work your way through the following chapters, I'm sure you'll want to listen to the results of the patching we've done, and to listen as you consider making your own changes to those patches. The output of all of the patches used in this book are set to direct their output to the default synth for your system. On the Macintosh, the default MIDI output is an AudioUnit DLS synthesizer. On Windows systems, the default MIDI output is the Microsoft DirectMusic DLS synthesizer.

You can see the destination used by the Max **noteout** object by double-clicking on the **noteout** object in a locked patch:

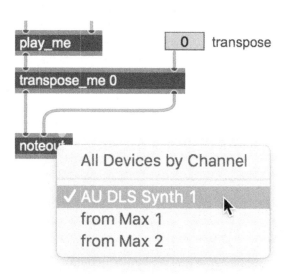

The *1* after the listing of the synth indicates that it's accepting input on
MIDI channel 1.

You may want to use something other than the default synth as you
work. The following sections demonstrate how you can load your own
softsynths, work with Max objects that will host VST/Audio Units plug-ins,
or work with Max for Live MIDI Instruments hosted by the Max **amxd~**
object.

Working With Softsynths

To use a softsynth, you'll need to launch it, and then choose one of the "from Max" destinations displayed when you double-click on the **noteout** object.

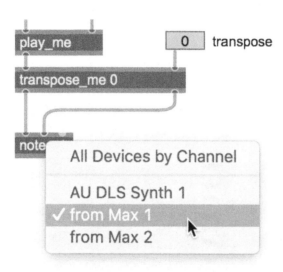

You should then configure your software synth's MIDI input to receive output from the "from Max" source you choose.

Working with VST/AU Synths

The *02_step_sequencer_VST* example patcher shows how to use the simple step sequencer with VST or Audio Units instrument plug-ins hosted by the MSP **vst~** object.

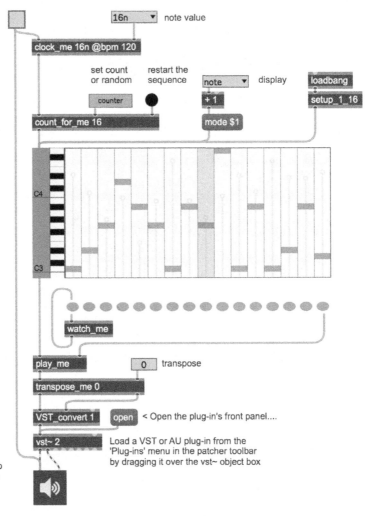

The only difference between this patcher and the original *01_simple_ step_sequencer* patch is right there at the bottom - a **vst~** object and another Max abstraction that replaces the **noteout** object in our original patch: the **VST_convert 1** abstraction.

This abstraction handles the task of taking output from our step sequencer patch and modifying the output into a form that the **vst~** object expects to receive. Here's what the inside of the **VST_convert 1** abstraction looks like:

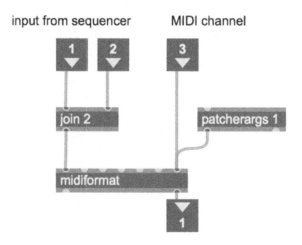

Sending output from our simple step sequencer isn't that difficult, but there is something we'll need to deal with: The **vst~** object expects to receive MIDI note information by means of a special message - the *midievent* message.

Happily, the Max **midiformat** object takes care of formatting those messages for us. In addition to doing normal MIDI message formatting, the right outlet of the **midiformat** object will output its messages in *midievent* message format – all we need to do is to use a **join 2** object to pack up the input messages and send the result on to the **midiformat** object. This isn't just a handy feature to have now – it will also be incredibly useful once you start doing other kinds of MIDI formatting (such as formatting messages for MIDI controllers or sending MIDI program change messages).

As you may have noticed, the **VST_convert 1** abstraction has an argument (*1*), just as we can see with the **transpose_me 0** patch. That means that we've added a **patcherargs 1** object to the abstraction to set an initial value for our MIDI output channel to 1.

Working With AMXD devices (for Max Users)

The *03_step_sequencer_AMXD* example patcher shows how to use the simple step sequencer with Max for Live instruments hosted by the Max **amxd~** object.

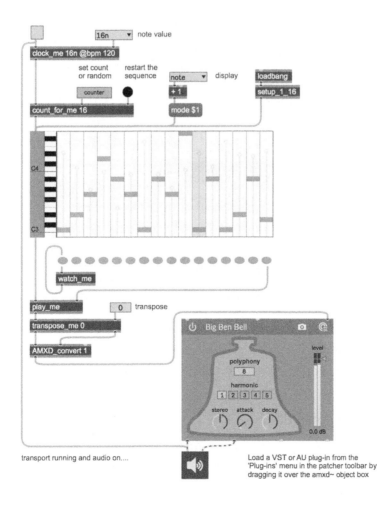

The difference between this patch and the one we used when hosting VST/AU plug-ins lies with the abstraction we use to take output from the **transpose_me 0** abstraction and convert it for use by the **amxd~** object – **AMXD_convert 1**.

The contents of the **AMXD_convert 1** abstraction are a little different from what we needed when working with the **vst~** object. See if you can spot the difference:

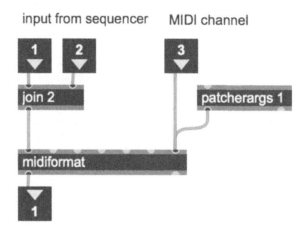

The difference is due to the fact that – unlike the **vst~** object, the **amxd~** object can accept ordinary **midiformat** object output in its right inlet, which means that we don't need to work with the *midievent* message.

We now have a basic step sequencer whose parts we understand, and a way to make some noise with the step sequencer. Let's start looking at other things we could do!

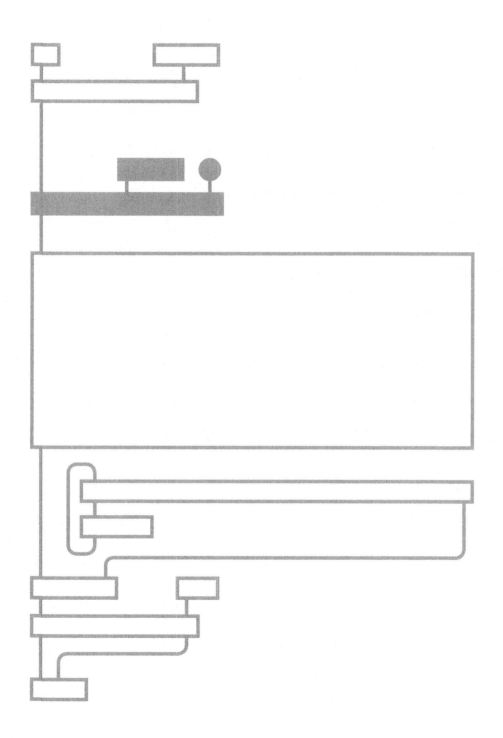

We're going to start building out our simple step sequencer with the part that tells you what step of your sequencer to fire next – the part that counts.

In this tutorial, we'll create some patches for generating and organizing variety based on the way that we do that counting. Since patching is always a personal practice, the collection of patches here embodies one of my favorite approaches: creating tools that don't try to do everything. Instead, I tend to make simple patches and then add to or modify them in the name of elegance or as the situation demands. This section involves creating four slightly different Max abstractions, each of which does something slightly different. They're all related along an evolutionary path, and I tend to use the one that fits my particular situation. Each one also can be a patch from which to start another patching idea.

In my own work, I have saved each of the four abstractions as a Max Snippet, which means I can easily add them from the patcher window as I work. Each of the four counter variants is included as a separate patch in this tutorial.

One Is The Loneliest Number

The first of our counting abstractions proceeds from the same basic idea. Counting sequentially by single steps is great, but why limit yourself to the very next step in your sequence?

Our simple step sequencer already lets us generate a random number between 1 and 16 and send that along to the **live.step** object for random output, but what else could we do? I'd like to show you one interesting possibility – counting by numbers other than one.

Here's a counting abstraction called **count_by**. It's pretty simple – you have a counting *range* (the number you count to), and you can set the amount you *count* by as well. When the result of your count falls outside of the value you want to count to, the result is wrapped and the count starts over. Here's what it looks like:

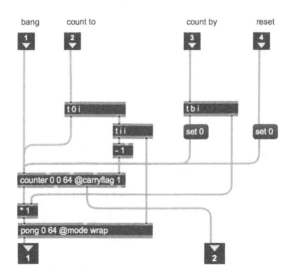

The insides are pretty straightforward – there's a **counter** object, but it's not handling the limits on counting – instead, it's giving us the number to multiply the count amount by, and we're using a **pong** object with its *@mode* attribute set to *wrap* to handle the boundary conditions and starting the count over. We're also using the **counter** object's *@carryflag* attribute to output a *bang* message rather than an integer.

The simple step sequencer patch itself only counts to 16, so why are the **counter** and the **pong** objects using a range of 0 to 64? There's a good reason for it – I wanted to set up my abstraction so that I can use it with *any* arbitrary range. The **live.step** object can handle sequences of up to 64 steps in length, so I've set the abstraction up using the maximum sequence – I can always set my default value of 16 steps in other ways (by using a **loadbang** object or by setting initial values for the **live.numbox** objects), and this makes my abstraction more generally useful.

The **count_by** abstraction uses **trigger** (**t**) objects liberally as a way to precisely sequence the initialization of the **counter** objects. We're also using it to allow us to reset the values when any of the inputs changes. Take a minute to look at the **trigger** objects in this abstraction and to follow what each one does. You'll see the **trigger** operation in use throughout this book, so getting familiar with how it works is a good idea.

Finally, you'll notice that the output of my abstraction runs in the range of 0 to 63. While most Max objects count starting from 0, the **live.step** object is different – it counts from 1 and expects numbers in the range of 1 to 64, So I'm going to have to add a 1 to the output. But you'll notice that I'm not doing that inside of the abstraction – instead, I'll adding 1 to the output of my abstraction in the parent patch itself.

While I *could* do the increment inside of my abstraction, adding that 1 in the parent patch means that I can use this same abstraction in other situations where I count from 0 instead 1. That makes this abstraction more broadly and generally useful – I can use my abstraction in *any* situation where I want to do some counting.

I'm going to add one final piece to my abstraction – something you've seen before. As you might imagine, it would be really nice to be able to set my initial values without a lot of mess and fuss for my patch. In the case of the simple step sequencer, I used the Max **patcherargs** object to allow me to set a default transposition value to my patch inside the abstraction. In that case, I was only going to be setting a single initial value. But this abstraction has several parameters, and it's not necessarily clear which one I would usually say first – it's just as easy to say "Count by twos to 16" as it is to say "Count to 16 by threes."

For this case (and the rest of the counting patches), I'm going to use the **patcherargs** object to let me add Max-style attributes to my subpatcher. Using the @-sign attribute method to identify the patcher arguments has a single great advantage: I can type the attributes in in any order I want. As the list of arguments gets longer, that's going to be really helpful.

Instead of a single **patcherargs** object, I'll also need a **route** object to for this abstraction, since I'm working with more than a single value. The **patcherargs** object lets me specify the name of the attributes I want using @-sign notation, and I can also provide a default value. When working with attributes, the **patcherargs** object sends attribute values out of its right output in the form of a set of two-item lists: the attribute name and its value. Adding a **route** object to the patch lets me select an attribute and send its value on to the proper location.

Here's what it looks like to add the **patcherargs** functionality to the
count_by abstraction and connect everything up:

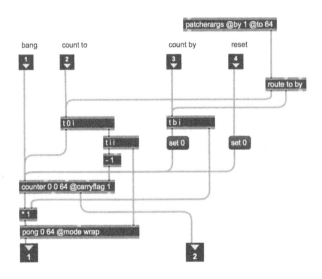

The archive of patches I've included with this tutorial has all of the
heavy lifting done for you. You can just initialize the abstractions with
arguments, and turn on the **metro** object to run the counts.

It's often the case that making a change to a patch has really interesting
results, and that's very much true here. Working with interesting counting
ranges and counting by more exotic numbers than 1 can yield some
interesting results.

Here are a few examples that you'll be able to see pretty easily (courtesy of an added **multislider** set to display ranges from 1 to 16):

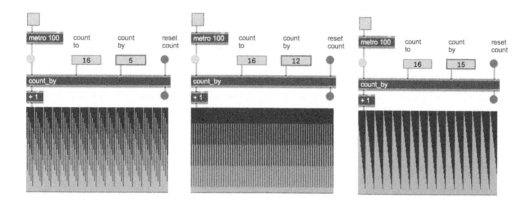

On A Roll

There's nothing wrong with the ordinary **counter** object in our original patch – it's also the heart of the **count_by** abstraction. But I'd like to add a few more features to allow me to riff through my sequences in different ways. As I go along, you may have some ideas of your own.

The judicious pairing of the **counter** and **pong** objects will be at the heart of all of the counting abstractions in this chapter. As I continue, I'm going to indicate the patching I've done to add functionality to my counting patches by highlighting the changes from the previous version. That way, you can more easily see the sequence of patching rather than just getting the result (and, I hope, you'll be able to see where you might make changes of your own).

My **count_by** abstraction lets me specify an upper bound and a count increment. While that's interesting, what if I added the ability to set a smaller region for my initial count within an overall range and then had the ability to move the starting position of that initial count by some amount?

It would look something like this:

                        1 2 3 4
                        2 3 4 5
                        3 4 5 6
                        4 5 6 1

Hey – that looks like a loop, doesn't it?

It turns out that adding that feature is not all too difficult – you just add another **counter** and **pong** object pair to create the larger range within which your original count occurs, and then trigger adding an increment (the amount of "roll") when you start the subcount over. You can use the standard **trigger**-centric way to handle initialization for the increment and range parameters.

Here's what the resulting **count_roll** abstraction looks like (with the new logic highlighted):

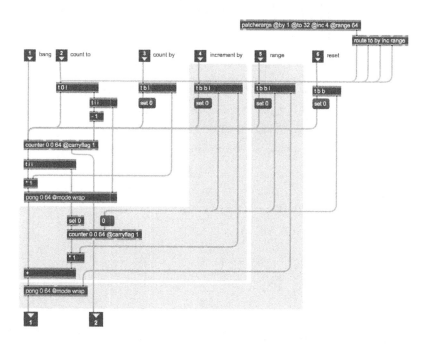

The result combines "*count by N*" approaches with content that can overlap or leap as you see fit:

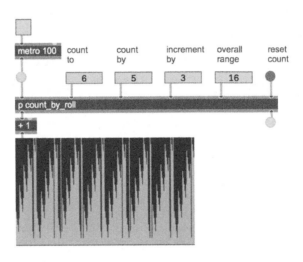

Rinse and Repeat

The successful looping/rolling count gives birth to the next idea – what about an abstraction that adds the ability to specify a specific *number* of repetitions of the subcount before doing the increment? That would give us loops that repeat a specified number of times.

Making that change is pretty straight-ahead: you add a **counter** object that keeps track of the number of repeats, incremented by the bang message output from the **counter** object that handles iterating through the subcount.

Here's what the **count_repeat** abstraction looks like:

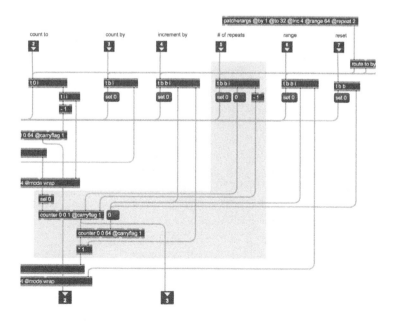

Adding this modification lets you start thinking of building larger repeating structures.

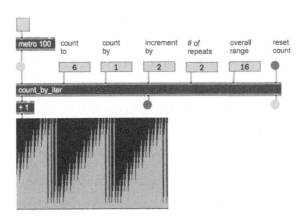

Know When To Fold `em

The final variation on the counting abstractions in this tutorial may have actually occurred to you while staring at the very first **count_by** abstraction. I can hear some of you saying, "Hey! You do know that the **pong** object will *fold* as well as wrap when it hits the limit you specify for it, right?"

That's absolutely true, and we now have two different places in our patch where we can choose to fold or wrap the count: the subcount, and the overall range. Making this change involves adding messages to the **pong** object that sets the object's boundary mode. Since the **pong** object expects to receive an integer to set its behavior – *mode 0* for wraps and *mode 1* for folds – we need to add a little logic to work with a UI object. We can use a **umenu**, or a **live.tab** or a **textbutton**.

In the interests of flexibility, I'm going to set my abstraction up so that it just takes an integer and constructs the message from there:

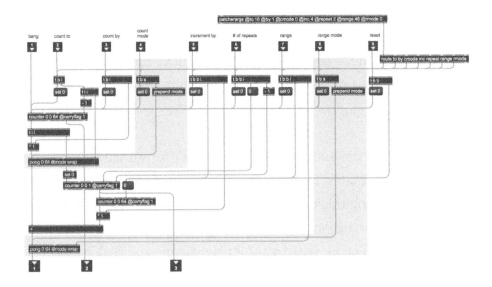

The result produces some amazing possibilities for generating various kinds of linear traversals.

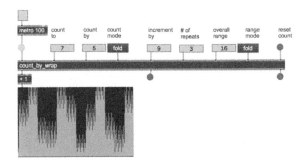

A Final Word

So there you have it: four interesting variations on ways to count in Max that you can tear apart and repurpose for your own projects. The patch folder for this chapter contains a patcher file called *count_on_it* that contains all four of these counting patchers. You can cut and paste them as needed. Each one can be substituted for the **counter** object's portion of the patch for the simple step sequencer.

The *counter_sequencer_patch* patch includes an example of how you might use it.

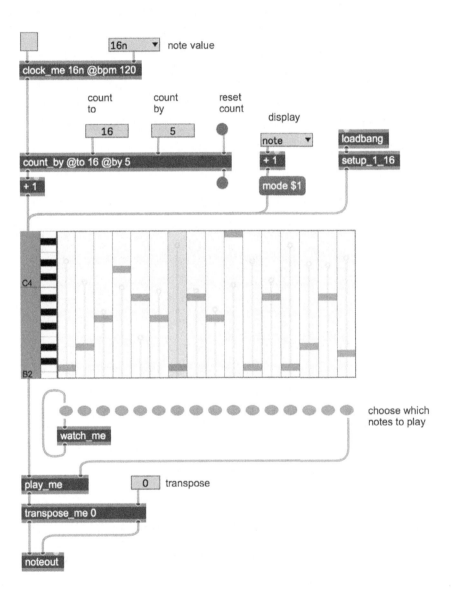

This finishes our first build-out of the simple step sequencer. Perhaps you can think of things you'd like to add – the ability to specify an initial offset for counting so that your sequencers start automatically on step 5 instead of step 1, for example (and have two **count_by** patchers running *together* to produce the same sequences offset by a controllable distance), or adding probabilistic random jumps in your count on command. The possibilities are endless.

You might consider using more than one of these counting patches to control another to generate greater variety – why not have a **count_by** patcher triggered by the *bang* outlets of a second **count_by** patcher to modify one of second object's parameters on the fly (say, to change the count increment)?

In our next chapter, we're going to look at the part of our simple step sequencer we're sending these numbers to – **live.step**, the heart of our sequencer.

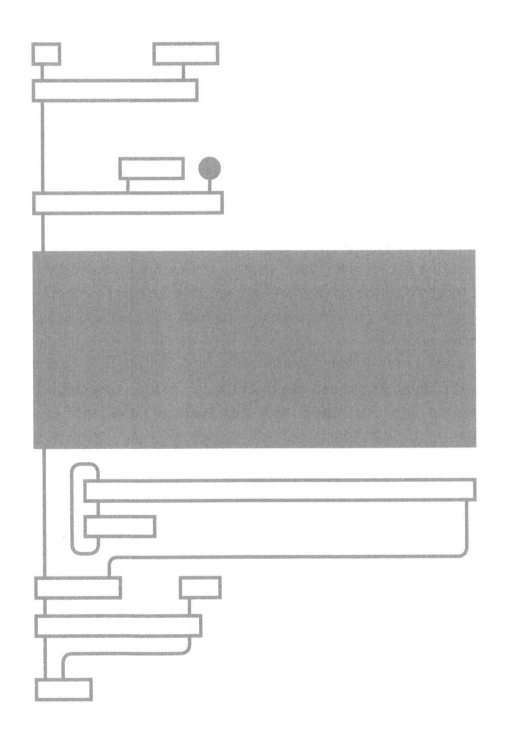

For this part of our examination of the step sequencer, we're going to do something that Max programmers do often: modify or build out their patches by taking advantage of features of a Max object that go beyond the default "vanilla" behavior of the object.

Max is full of external objects that are not only useful in their default state, but also provide deep and subtle functionality to the user willing to explore them. In particular, we'll be taking the first of several looks at the part of our simple sequencer patch that stores the note or event data associated with a step in a sequence – the **live.step** object.

It's likely that a good number of you have run into the **live.step** object as a part of Darwin Grosse's elegant and lovely Max For Live Step Sequencer MIDI device, or perhaps you've spent a few enjoyable minutes messing about with the multi-tabbed help file. For this chapter, I'm going to start simple, run down a few of the object's features, and teach it a few tricks.

The **live.step** object is a great interface for working with short sequences – you can view and edit sequences using the object's user interface while your sequence is running. The object also helpfully includes some "extra" events beyond the normal note/velocity/duration triplets you normally use to construct MIDI messages associated with steps in the sequence – you can use those extra messages for anything you'd like.

The **live.step** object drops into your patch with a rich feature set and lots of cool options for UI design all ready to go – you can fire up the object's help file and just vanish for a few pleasant hours. I invite you to do so when we're finished here, in fact.

Keeping it Simple

At its heart, the **live.step** object provides a simple way to enter, play, and edit monophonic sequences for Max and Max for Live users. The *01_live_step_overview* patch shows a very simple example of the **live.step** object at work outside of our step sequencer, and will introduce you to a few simple control messages.

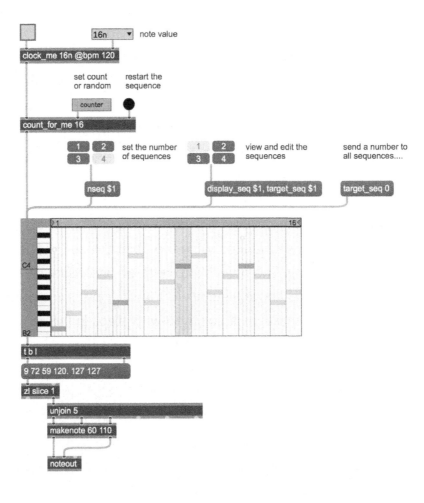

The **live.step** object lets you store up to 16 monophonic sequences. Each sequence can have between 1 and 64 steps. Each step is composed of five values that we can use to specify MIDI-style pitch and velocity (0 - 127), a duration value (128 values in the range 0 - 960, quantized in increments of 7.5), and a pair of "extra" parameters also in the range of 0 - 127 that you can use for anything you'd like.

The *01_live_step_overview* patch's **live.step** object stores 4 sequences of 16 steps. As with the simple step sequencer patch, we've set it up for use with your favorite softsynth or Max for Live device by way of a pair of Max MIDI objects (**makenote** and **noteout**), and we're also using the same basic **clock_me** and **count_for_me** abstraction pair to drive sequence playback.

You can take a listen to the four sequences by firing up a softsynth, setting the **noteout** object's output to match what your softsynth expects, and then clicking on the **toggle** attached to the **count_for_me** abstraction to start playing the first sequence.

How does the **live.step** object know how many sequences it has stored? That's set using the *nseq* message. In the *live_step_overview* patch, the number of sequences is initially set to 4 using a Max **tab** object. You might also be asking yourself how you can view the other sequences. There are two messages that help us do that:

1. The message *target_seq <sequence-number>* chooses which sequence we want to be playing back.

2. The message *display_seq <sequence-number>* chooses which
sequence we want to view as part of the **live.step** object's display.

To see each of the four stored sequences, click on the tab object
attached to the **message** box containing *display_seq $1, target_seq $1*.
Clicking on one of the numbers will choose it for playback, and display
the sequence. You can also edit the currently displayed sequence while
it's playing, too.

If you're doing a little exploring on your own, you've probably figured out
that the *nseq* message and the *display_seq* and *target_seq* messages
interact with one another – the *nseq* message sets the number of
possible sequences that can be accessed using the *display_seq* and
target_seq messages. If you set the number of sequences to 2 (i.e. by
sending the message *nseq 2*), you'll only be able to display and edit the
first two sequences.

So here's how the rest of our example patch works:

- The sequencer-counter subpatch counts in a cycle between 1 and
  16, and sends that integer to the **live.step** object.

- When the **live.step** object receives that integer, it outputs a message
  composed of the number it received followed by the five stored
  values (pitch/velocity/duration/extra1/extra2) for the numbered step
  in the sequence.

- The *01_live_step_overview* patch uses a *zl slice 1* object to peel off
  the first number from the list.

- An **unjoin 5** object is then used to grab the first three items in the remaining list (the MIDI note number, velocity, and duration messages) that it then sends to a **makenote** object to construct MIDI note messages.

That's a basic subset of the **live.step** object's functionality. Now, let's teach it a few new tricks.

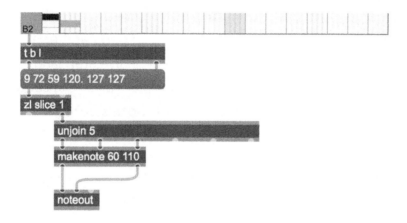

Polyphony?

The ability to use a message to specify a specific instance of stored data from among a set is something you've probably run into before in a slightly different form if you're making your way in the Max world – the **poly~** object.

The **poly~** object (and its cousin **poly**) let you use a *target 0* message when you want to talk to all instances of the loaded patcher at the same time. That's also true for the **live.step** object. In **live.step** land, the *target_seq 0* message has a similar effect in that it plays **all** of the sequences at the same time – actually it plays as many of those stacked sequences as you specify using the nseq *<number>* message.

Click on the **message** box containing the message *target_seq 0* and listen to what happens. You'll hear polyphonic playback, and the number of simultaneous voices you hear will depend on the total number of sequences you've specified using the *nseq* message. Presto – instant polyphonic sequencing!

Of course, the minute you send the *display_seq/target_seq* pair, you're back to one note per step.

Although the *nseq* message can be used to select the number of the stored sequences to play back all at once, it seems kind of a shame that we have only two options (i.e. one sequence or all of them). Let's do a little Max patching and rectify that situation.

The 02_rotating_groups patch provides an example of how we might work with large stacks of sequences – in this case, 8 sequences of 16 steps each. You'll notice a few changes from the overview patch: the addition of a **pattern_rotator** abstraction, which lets you use a **umenu** object to select a pattern of sequences from the collection to play (and does something else interesting that we'll talk about later), a **matrixctrl** object that displays the sequences currently being played, and the **sequence_select** abstraction, which handles turning the selected sequence steps on and off for playback.

While the *01_live_step_overview* patch used a **message** box to display
the message that the **live.step** object spits out each time it receives an
integer between 1 and 16, we've added a **print** object to the patch to
show you what target_seq 0 output really looks like.

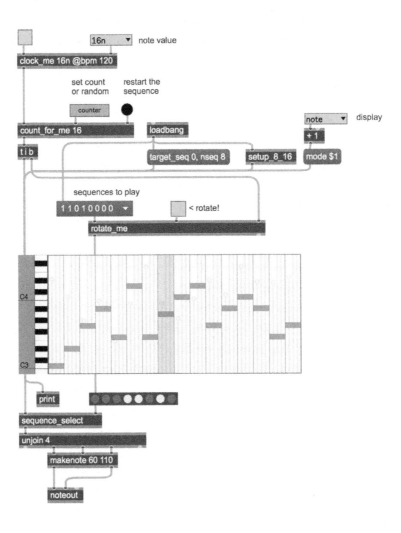

Click on the *target_seq 0, nseq 8* message box again to make sure you've enabled polyphonic output and then open the Max window and take a look at the output being sent to the **print** object.

Select a pattern of sequence playback from the **umenu** item labeled "sequences to play" and start the transport.

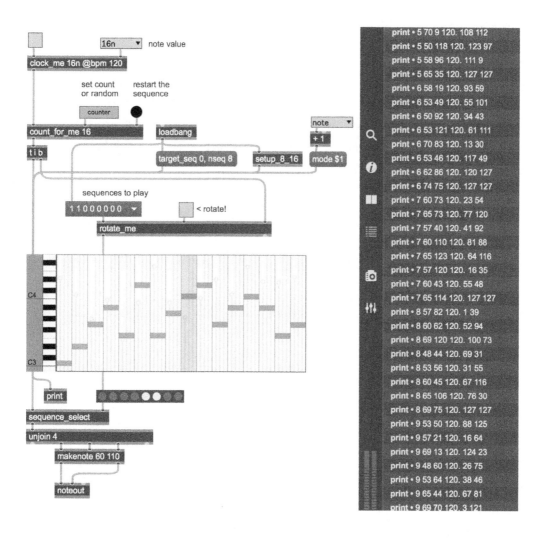

While the **message** box/**trigger** object pair in the sample patch shows only one message at a time, the **print** object shows that the **live.step** object is sending out several similar messages for every integer received – one message for the step of each sequence in our collection of sequences stored in the **live.step** object. Now that we know that, we can start patching to do something interesting.

But how can we take a look at the individual sequences in the stack (or edit them)?

The 02_rotating_groups patch contains an abstraction called **sequence_select** that collects all the messages output by sending a single integer to the **live.step** object and splitting them up into eight individual groups of note message data that we can switch on and off while our sequence is running. This patcher really shows the **zl** family of Max objects in action.

Here's what's going on inside of the **sequence select** abstraction:

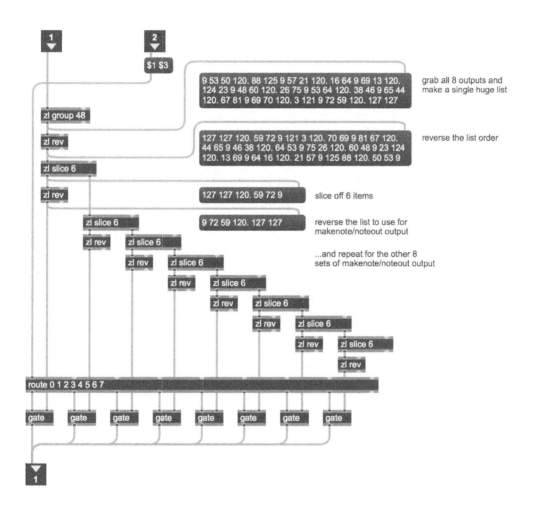

This abstraction takes all eight messages (one for each sequence in our collection for a given step) and then concatenates them into a single large message using a **zl group** object. We'll break them up into separate messages as we go along.

One result of doing this is that collecting the list will give us all the events
in the *reverse* order (last in/first out), while we want to be able to work
with the component parts in first-to-last order (i.e.sequence 1, then
sequence 2, etc.). We can solve that problem by taking our large message
and reversing it using a **zl rev** object it so that the note events are in the
correct order.

After that, it's a simple matter to slice the large message into increasingly
smaller units using a **zl slice 6** object and peeling off each of the six
events and then reversing that list, in turn. A set of **gate** objects then
allows us to enable or disable the output of any of the six outputs.

The **rotate_me** abstraction takes a list of eight zeros and ones (from
the middle outlet of the **umenu** object), sets the **matrixctrl** object to
reflect the selection, and passes the list along to the **sequence_select**
abstraction that we just examined. We'll look at it in detail next.

A Little Animation

The **rotate_me** abstraction has another interesting feature – the ability to *rotate* the pattern of zeros and ones while the sequence is playing to add variety to the polyphonic playback. The rotation is controlled by the **toggle** attached to the **pattern_rotator** abstraction (turn it on and listen to what happens).

Let's look at how the **rotate_me** abstraction does its work:

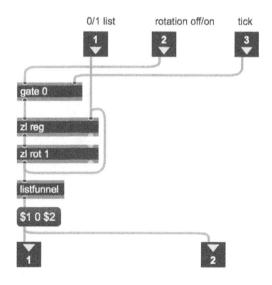

This abstraction makes use again of the **zl** family of objects to store a list received in the patcher's left inlet, and a **zl** family object you may not have seen before – a **zl rot 1** object. The object stores any list it receives, and will rotate the list items "forward" one position (as set by the argument to the object) when it receives a *bang* message.

Since we want to turn the rotation off and on, the patcher includes
a **gate 0** object that we use to assure that no *bang* messages to perform
the rotation will be sent on to the **trigger** object when rotation is turned
off.

The newly rotated list is then sent to a **listfunnel** object that does
something simple but really useful: it outputs each item in the list as an
indexed list whose first index is 0 (this object counts from zero, which is
what the **matrixctrl** object awaiting its output expects).

The only thing we need to do to that output is to put another zero
between the first and second items in our list – the **matrixctrl** object
expects to get a message that is a list of 3 items – the column (horizontal
position) of a **matrixctrl** "switch", the row for the switch, and the
value from the original list. A **message** box **$1 0 $2** uses standard Max $
notation to take the list from the **listfunnel** object's output and add that
middle zero. When the gate is turned off, the second **message** box lets
you use the **umenu** item to pass an unrotated pattern through.

Food For Thought

Of course, there's more interesting work that could be done with this patch.

- We're triggering the rotation of the collection of sequences from the same counter that controls the **live.step** object. What if the rotation had its own counter?

- The **zl rot 1** object that does the rotation only rotates by single steps. We could redo our patcher so that it can rotate forward and backward, and do so by values other than a single rotation.

- We can add the ability to "step through" the patterns stored in the **umenu** object by adding a **counter** object there, too.

There are a lot of possibilities left to be explored here.

In a future chapter on the **live.step** object, we'll be spending a little time thinking about going long – working in odd-length sequences composed of unusual total length.

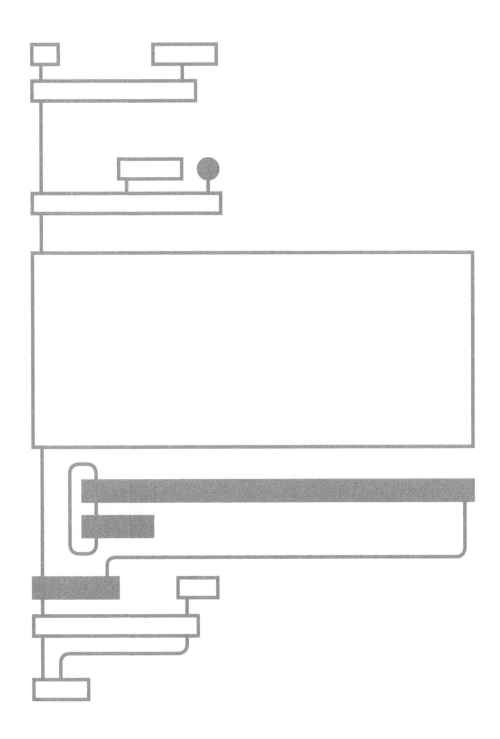

Assumptions are unavoidable.

We make them all the time – assumptions are the "safe place" from which we proceed when we imagine something new, or start work, or simply walk into a room full of people we've never met. The problem is that assumptions may not always be accurate, or that clinging to them means we'll miss something. One good general strategy is to try to be aware of our assumptions – to think *about* what you're thinking *with*.

That practice extends to patching, too – where it can be an interesting spur to creativity.

We've been thinking of the idea of a step sequencer as being composed of some simple and basic parts:

· A counter that tells us what step of the sequencer to trigger,

· A bunch of events or data that correspond to MIDI notes

This time out, we're going to think about another of those pieces – the part of our patch that lets us add variety by means of the ability to turn any note in our sequence "on" or "off." I initially added it to my first Max sequencer because one of my hardware sequencers had that ability (see what I mean about assumptions?).

Creativity is often all about starting with assumptions and then trying to make new ones, and then riffing off those assumptions, in turn. Here's an example: Here are two very different assumptions we've made so far with our simple sequencer when it comes to note events:

- We've decided that any note event our sequencer produces will face one of two possible outcomes: it'll be played, or it won't. And we can decide ahead of time how that will happen.

- We've made another and more subtle assumption, however – the ordering of the functional units in our simple sequencer patch itself makes some assumptions about what's going to happen and how.

In this section, we're going to think about both of those ideas, and create ways to teach our simple sequencer some new tricks.

Heads Or Tails?

In a way, we've already gotten a little creative with our simple sequencer patch – many hardware and software sequencers don't have a provision for choosing to output a note for a specific position in a sequence. Instead of the note events being gated for individual steps, everything is output. One way we can build out our original patch is to create a way to vary the output as we go when determining whether or not a given step in a sequence will be played.

Here's a really simple "flip of a coin" way to do that using a Max object that does, in fact, do the Max version of coin-flipping – the **decide** object.

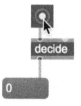

The object is simplicity itself – whenever a **decide** object receives a *bang* message, it outputs a zero or one. The following little Max patch provides a way to show you how the **decide** object works over time – over the course of a lot of coin-flipping:

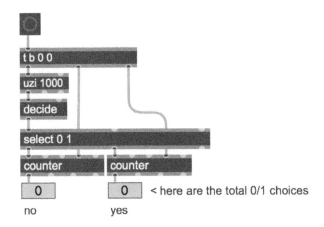

Pressing the **button** object at the top sets the **counter** object to zero, and then sends 1000 *bang* messages to the **decide** object. Each time the object receives a *bang* message, it flips a coin and outputs a zero or one. As you can see, by pressing the button lots of times, those 1000 outcomes aren't always 50/50 (although they hover around that number).

We can use that zero or one output in conjunction with Max's **gate** object to create a mini patch that will randomly decide whether or not to produce output (or "play"). The *01_coin_flipping_sequencer* patch is an example of that approach.

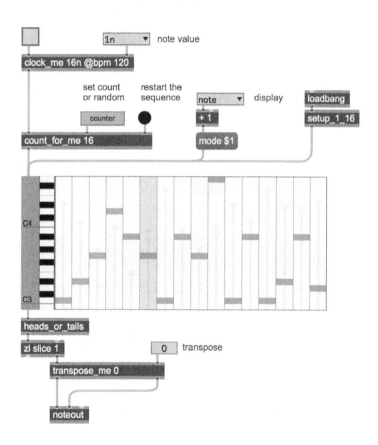

This simple variation on our original sequencer patch makes a very few modifications – it replaces the matrixctrl object and **play_me** abstraction with a new abstraction – **heads_or_tails**.

Let's double-click to look inside the patcher.

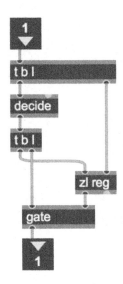

The normal four-item list of numbers from the **live.step** object is received and sent to a **trigger** object that does two things having to do with lists and *bang* messages (those are indicated in the trigger object by the l and **b** arguments:

- It sends the list (l) on to the right inlet of a **zl reg** object, which works like a sample-and-hold unit: it will store any number or list we give it and then output it the next time it receives a *bang* message.

- After sending the list on, it sends a *bang* message (**b**) to our **decide** object, which will output either a zero or one.

That result is sent to another **trigger** object that does two things:

1. First, it sends the one or zero to a **gate** object, which will then open or close the gate for the next input it receives in its right inlet

2. The second **trigger** object then sends a *bang* message to the **zl reg** object that's currently holding that 4-item list.

Again – take note of those two **trigger** objects in this patcher – they reliably handle setting up a specific order of operations in the Max patch and making sure that they always happen in a fixed order.

One subtle feature worth pointing out here: We're assuming that the **heads_or_tails** abstraction is working with lists (the second argument to the **trigger** object in the patcher tells us that, and we're using the **zl reg** object to store our list). A neat feature of this bit of patching is that it'll work if we send it lists or an integer or a floating-point value, too – integers or floating-point numbers are treated as a *list with only one item*. That makes our patcher more generally useful – always a good thing to think about when you're patching.

You'll notice that our modified simple sequencer patch also includes a **zl slice 1** object connected to the output of the **heads_or_tails** abstraction. We've added it because the list received from the **live. step** object has a number as its first item that indicates the number of the sequence step. In the original **play_me** abstraction, we used that information, but we don't need it in this patcher at all. We use a **zl slice** object to slice the first item off our four-item list and pass the rest of the list along by sending it out the right outlet.

What's the Chance of
That Happening?

It's amazing how much of a difference making such a simple change makes in the sequencer's output – the variations in note events being played preserves the musical content of the sequence, but presents it with variations on every cycle.

I'm sure that you're reading along and starting to wonder how you could set the *likelihood* of the note being output instead of always having it be the result of a flip of the coin. The *02_random_percentage_sequencer* patch implements that ability.

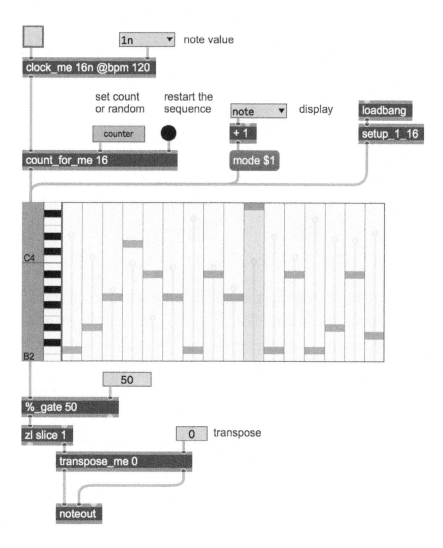

We can modify the patch we just created and swap out the **heads_or_ tails** abstraction we made for a new one – the **%_gate 50** abstraction to do that. Here's what's inside:

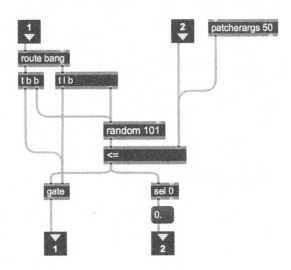

This patcher looks a little more complicated than our original, but here's what's happening: The abstraction accepts a percentage value (between 0 and 100) in its second inlet to set the likelihood that we'll send the input along along. It receives the standard list of MIDI note data from the **live.step** object as before, and then uses the **random 101** object to choose a number every time a new list arrives. The **<=** object tests the random number in relation to the percentage we specify. If the random number is equal to or less than the threshold, the **gate** object opens up and the input list will be sent along, If not, all will be still and quiet.

Since you've been paying close attention, you will no doubt have noticed that there's going to be a problem with the list that's sent from the **live.**

step object: we need to strip the event number from the list in order to isolate the MIDI note message information, and that's not being done anywhere inside the patcher. As with the *01_coin_flipping_sequencer* patch, we're adding a **zl slice 1** object outside of the patcher to do the work. There's a good reason for that – and it also explains why we have the **route bang** and **t b b** objects and the second outlet, too.

What's that **route bang** object doing in the abstraction, anyway? The **%_gate 50** abstraction is an example of a simpler patch that's had something added to it to make the abstraction more generally useful – something we'll be doing all the way through this book. Let me explain.

I initially had a simpler patch that looked like this:

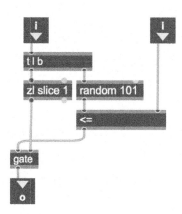

It worked just fine for lists from the **live.step** object. But as I looked at it, I realized that this was a patch that I could use in other ways, too. Since integers and floats are nothing more than lists with only one item, my patcher would also work as a percentage-based gate for numbers and Jitter matrices. In fact, the *only* kind of Max message my little patcher wouldn't work with was *bang* messages. I had the beginnings of a real "Swiss Army Knife" of a patcher.

By adding a **route bang** object, I could grab *bang* messages and then sequence and pass them along (using the **t b b** object), and then anything else would be sent out the **route** object's right inlet. Making that slight change gave me a **%_gate** abstraction that I could use anywhere in Max in the future.

There's one more specific difference in this patch that renders it less useful in a general situation – the **zl slice 1** object needs to be there when working with **live.step** output lists, but that won't *always* be something I need. In the interests of remaining general, it's smarter to do the list slicing in my larger patch outside of the patcher. It's a similar situation we encountered in working with counters in the second chapter – since **live.step** counts from one instead of zero, we took the generalized counter abstractions and added one to their output in the parent patch.

By now, I'm sure you know why I added a **patcherargs** object to my patcher – it lets me specify an initial testing value for my patcher by typing an argument into the patcher's object box (e.g. **%_gate 50**).

But what about that right outlet to the patcher? As I thought about other things I might do with my patcher, I realized that it'd be a nice idea to be able to visualize what my patcher was doing as it worked. Since it only passed output when the random number passed the percentage test, the only output the original patcher produced was the successful output.

Adding a **sel 0** object and a **message** box containing a value of 0. Would send a value of *0.* out that right outlet when the test failed, providing me with a way to visualize the density of the patcher's output.

Now, I can provide a simple way to show you how the **%_gate** abstraction works that'll make what's going on inside a lot clearer. The *percentage_density* patch shows a visual example of the **%_gate** abstraction in action, demonstrating how that percentage setting changes the density of event output (we're using random numbers here instead of MIDI messages, but the patcher passes that along, too). This might be useful for future UI work later on.

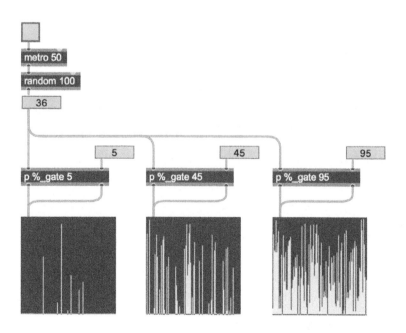

Location Location Location

Now that we have an interesting way to control output using probabilities, it's time to take a look at one of our other assumptions – one we haven't considered at all: *the ordering of the data that flows from one "functional unit" of the patch to another*.

When we patch in Max on an object-to-object level, we're always thinking about the flow of data and the order in which things happen – it's one of the reasons why we love the **trigger** object so much. But when it comes to working at higher levels – say, conceiving of a patch as a series of basic operations – it's easy to forget that making similar changes at different places in your patch can make a world of difference.

The *location_location* patcher provides an example of this. We now have a way to set the probability that an event will be passed through unaltered. That's pretty cool. And the great thing is that our little **%_gate** abstraction is an all-purpose device: it will pass integers, floats, and lists and bang messages with no alteration.

The patch uses the **%_gate 50** abstraction in two different places in our simple sequencer, with two very different results:

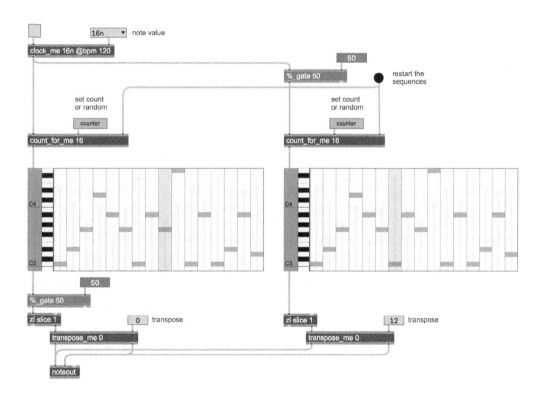

If you look carefully, you can see that there's a **%_gate** abstraction used in two different places in the patch. The **metro** object is driving what is essentially two versions of the very same patch. In the left version of the sequencer, the **%_gate** abstraction is sitting where we initially placed it, making a probabilistic decision whenever a new list of numbers arrives whether to pass the list on or not.

The right portion of the patcher is a little different, though – in this case, the **%_gate** abstraction is located between the **metro** object and the **counter**. When the patcher is used at the top of the sequencer patch, the probabilistic output will determine whether a *bang* message is sent to the **counter** object – the result being that the sequencer doesn't "skip a step" when the **metro** sends a **bang** message. Instead, the patcher sets a probability that the step sequencer will move to the next step.

When the patcher is used farther down in the sequencer, the probabilistic output will determine whether or not a step in the sequence will be "skipped" or not.

To help you hear the difference between the two patches, the step sequencer on the right is transposed up an octave. In the left portion, the melody is punctuated by rests, but it still repeats every 16 beats; in the right portion every note is played, but delays are introduced which make it longer and shift it out of sync with the left portion of the patch.

The resulting output from this simple programming choice provides very different results, and you – as the programmer – get to choose the one that you find most appealing. As you work, you might want to keep ideas like this in the back of your mind. For example, you could combine this patcher with the step sequencer's original logic that let us turn individual steps in the sequence off or on. When we do that, a step which is "on" will also not necessarily be one that sounds, depending on the patcher's decision to pass the event on or not.

Playing The Odds

Now that we have the **%_gate** abstraction, we can consider modifying our simple sequencer patch further. We can replace the bank of on/off switches with the ability to set a percentage likelihood that any individual step in the sequence will be played – think of it as a modification of our original bank of on/off switches.

This is one of the places where the habit of generalizing your Max patchers and abstractions really pays off. Let's take a look again at the inside of the **play_me** abstraction from our original simple sequencer patch:

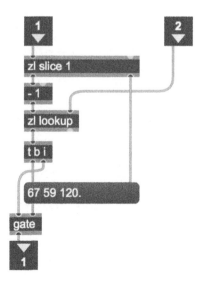

When it came to controlling the **gate** object that passed or prevented messages from getting through in this patcher, we took a list of zero and one values, and then stepped through the sequence by grabbing the *nth* item from that list and using it to open and close our **gate** object. The nice thing here is that we can think of that list as also being something we can work with if we have a list of percentage values that are used to determine whether or not a step will be output. We can take the patching we already have and modify it so that it will let us create a patch that replaces the on/off switches with percentages for each step in the sequence. All we need to do is to add in the random number generation and testing logic from the **%_gate** abstraction.

We'll call our new abstraction **%_play_me**. Here's what that looks like:

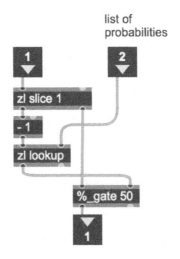

Pretty simple, and this demonstrates the advantage of doing the general-case patching in the **%_gate 50** abstraction we created earlier. All we have to do is to slice the event number from an incoming list using the **zl slice 1** object, and then use that number to index a list of numbers in the range 0 – 100 (one item for each step in the sequence). The *nth* item output from the **zl lookup** object gives us the percentage probability for that note.

The only change to the outside of our simple sequencer patch involves adding a UI for setting the individual values. For the *03_percentage_gates_sequencer* patch, we will use **live.numbox** objects attached to a **join 16 @triggers –1** object. The *@triggers -1* attribute sets the join object to send its contents to the **%_play_me 50** abstraction if any of the **live.numbox** objects are changed.

Here's what the final result looks like:

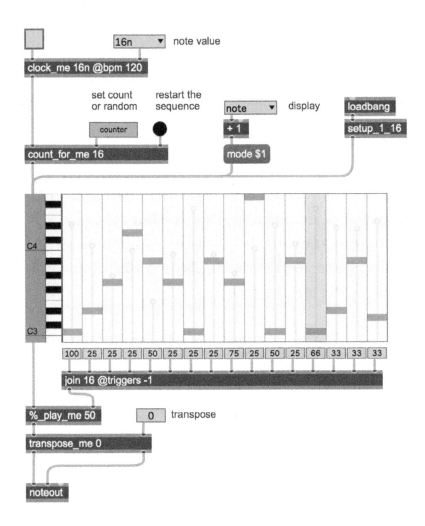

The three example patches in this chapter all provide ways to add variety to the output of your step sequencer. Of course, there are lots of other interesting ways to decide whether to play a note in your step sequencer. In a later chapter, we'll look at a few other interesting and more exotic variations.

Questions of Scale(s):
Transposition and Mapping

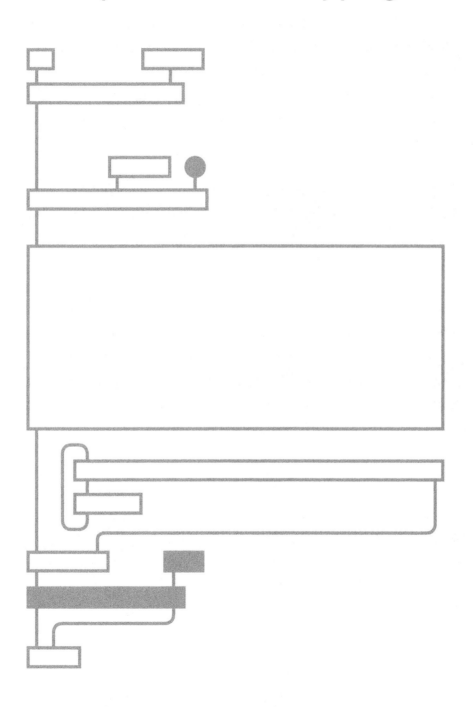

One of the things that makes Max great to work with is the ability to have a patch running *while you're writing it* – having numbers and lists and messages moving around in real time and doing real things. Working with Max is often a question of learning to map outputs to inputs – knowing how to change output from one part of a Max patch so that it works with the input of another part of the patch.

Transposition is one form of mapping that every musician is familiar with. We think about it every time we change an arrangement to fit into a range we can sing or play in, or every time we think about moving between one musical scale or key to another.

In this chapter, we're going to look at transposition in our step sequencer – the practice of mapping one set of outputs (in this case, from our sequencer patch) to another to create new scales, modes, and new melodies and patterns. Our original simple step sequencer patch had some transposition capabilities built into it already, which suggests just how basic the ability to perform that kind of mapping is.

The **transpose_me** abstraction in our original step sequencer patch was simplicity itself:

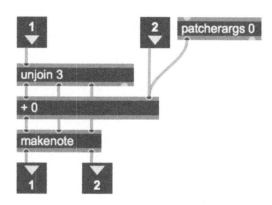

The abstraction took the MIDI note/velocity/duration list of values and separated them into separate elements. It then took the MIDI note number and performed a simple transposition of that input by adding or subtracting from the original MIDI note number's value. Finally, the Max **makenote** object was used to format a pair of MIDI note-on and note-off messages to be passed on as output to a software or hardware synth.

That kind of simple numeric transposition works better for transposing by some intervals than for others. While fifths (+ 7), fourths (+5), and even sevenths (- 1) all work pretty well, there are still places where the notes in your sequence will no longer be in the place you expect – you were expecting a G and you got an F# instead because you were adding numbers rather than thinking about the scale you wanted to use. For other transposition values, that'll be a lot more noticeable – more notes will not be where you want them to be.

In this tutorial, we'll be looking at some options related to what we have started out thinking of as transposition. But we're really talking about a more general Max topic: mapping – setting up a pattern of transformations we can apply to a range of inputs that will give us an output we find pleasing.

Note Filtering

One modification we can make to our simple sequencing involves the process of filtering MIDI notes – pre-specifying which MIDI notes we want to work with, and having our patch omit any other MIDI notes it receives (think of it as something similar to our ability to pre-select which steps in a sequence we wished to output in our original step sequencer).

The Max patch *01_transpose_filter* demonstrates this technique:

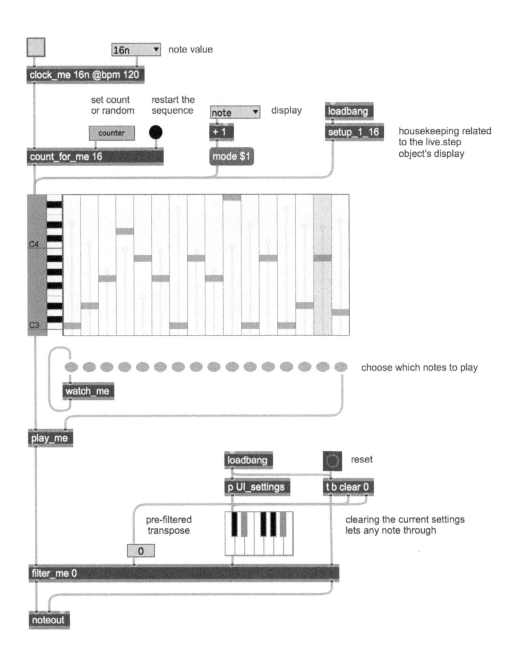

This patch replaces the original **transpose_me** abstraction with a new one– **filter_me 0** – which includes a user interface that lets you click on notes on a keyboard to "turn them off" (i.e. to omit them from being played).

The patcher requires a little Max "housekeeping" patching for initialization and providing us with the means to reset our transpositions and filtering. As with many Max UI objects, we use messages to configure their look and behavior. The **UI_settings** abstraction sets up the Max **kslider** object for our use.

Here's a look at the inside of the patcher (which runs every time we open the patch, courtesy of a **loadbang** object:

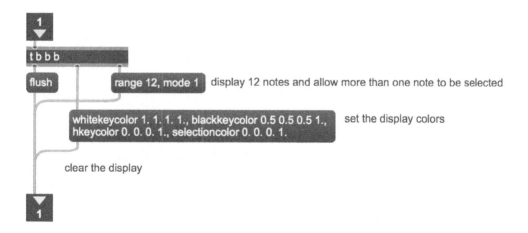

When we launch our patch, the **UI_settings** abstraction sends several messages to the Max **kslider** object, in the order specified by using our friend the **trigger** object. Here they are, in order:

1. The **kslider** object is set to display a range of 12 notes.

2. The **kslider** object is configured so that we can select more than one note on the keyboard display at a time by clicking on it (*mode 1*).

3. Four messages are sent to the **kslider** object to set the colors used when displaying the keyboard. We set colors for the black and white keys when they are not clicked on (*whitekeycolor 1. 1. 1. 1.* and *blackkeycolor 0.5 0.5 0.5 1.*), a color to use when a key has initially clicked on *selectioncolor 0. 0. 0. 1.*) and one when it's been "turned off" after it's been selected (*hkeycolor 0. 0. 0. 1.*).

4. The **kslider** object's display is cleared using the *flush* message.

The main patch also includes a **button – t b clear 0** object combination to manually reset both the pre-filtered transposition value and the **filter_ me** abstraction-**kslider** object combination.

Although it's large, the contents of the **filter_me** abstraction will look somewhat familiar to you by now.

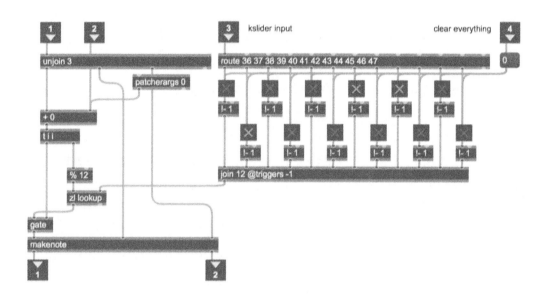

The left-hand portion of the patcher closely resembles previous patchers intended to parse a MIDI note message and to perform some action based its content. Once the message is parsed using the unjoin object, we use a Max **%12** object to identify what the note name is and then use that number as an index to a **zl lookup** object to select the on/off state of that particular note. If the twelve-item list of zeros and ones indicates that the note is in our selected scale or set of notes, a **gate** object is opened and the note number is passed through.

The right-hand portion of the patcher is used to construct the 12-item list of ones and zeros based on input from the **kslider** object, which outputs MIDI note numbers in the range from 36 to 47 whenever the key is clicked on.

When we click on a key in the **kslider**, we're indicating that we don't want to pass the note. To do this, we use a standard bang message to a **toggle** object to set the value and add a **!= 1** object to invert the result – so when the **route** object matches the key we've clicked on in the **kslider**, it sets its list item to zero. Whenever the **kslider** display is changed, the right-hand part of the patcher outputs the twelve-item list of zero and one values used to gate incoming MIDI note numbers.

The best way to get a sense of how transposing the **live.step** object's output interacts with the **kslider**-based note filter is to try it. Start the sequencer up and listen to the unfiltered results. Now, click on the notes C#, E, F#, G# and B to filter them from the output (you won't hear any effect of this since none of those notes appears in the sequence currently stored in the **live.step** object. Now, click on the **number box** labeled "pre-filtered transpose," enter a number and listen to how the output changes.

You'll notice that some numbers (say, 5, 7, and 10) result in more notes being output than others (try 1, 6, or 11). That's the result of combining numerical transposition with note filtering – you can transpose your sequence in such a way that far fewer step sequencer events will be played because the transposed note values fall outside of the note values you've specified.

Scales and Modes

When it comes to making decisions on note output, lots of musicians are used to thinking modally – using patterns of whole and half steps from a given starting note (which defines the "key" for the scale or mode) to express a particular scale. For the next step in building out from our simple sequencer patch, we'll make some modifications to the patch we just created to let us specify scales or modes and transpositions for our sequencer output.

Here's the *02_transpose_scalemode* patch, which lets us set scales and modes for transposition:

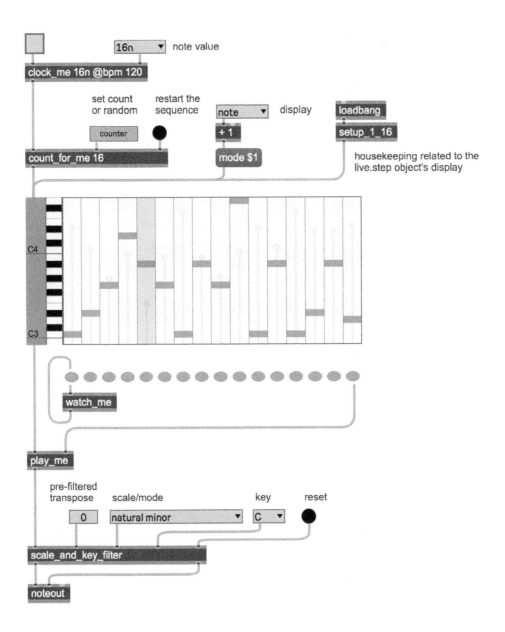

The difference lies in how the **scale_and_key_filter** abstraction creates the pattern of *0* and *1*. In addition, we've included the contents of the **scale_me** abstraction we just looked at as part of this patcher

Let's take a look at the inner workings of the **scales_and_key_filter** abstraction:

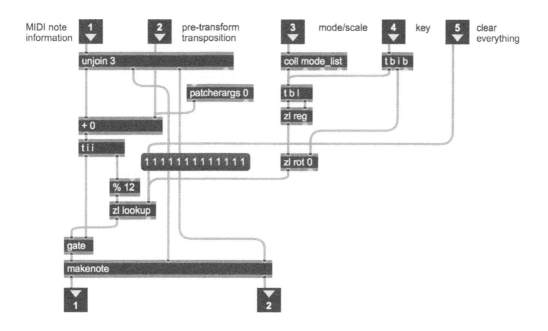

You'll recognize the left-hand portion of this patch, since it's the same patching we used in the previous example. This patcher sets the pattern of zeros and ones used to pass MIDI note events in a different way – two **live.menu** objects in the parent patch are used to set a scale or mode and a key signature for the output filter.

This portion of the patch features a Max object we haven't seen at all so far in this book – a Max object in wide use in many data storage situations: the Max **coll** (collection) object. This deep and subtle Max object lets you store, organize, retrieve, and edit collections of different messages.

While it has a lot of features, the **coll** object we're using here does something fairly simple: it stores a set of lists of zeros and ones (does this sound familiar?) that correspond to the notes associated with a scale or mode. For the sake of convenience, we have used the coll object's Inspector to set the *Save Data with Patcher* option for the **coll mode_list** object.

There is one entry for each of the scales/modes listed in the **live.menu** item. When you choose a scale or mode from the **live.menu** object in the parent patch, an integer value corresponding to the scale or mode pattern is sent to the **coll mode_list** object, which outputs the zero/one pattern list that corresponds to the mode you select.

To see the contents of the **coll** object, you can double-click on the object to display its contents.

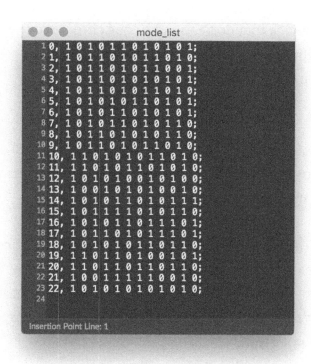

The **coll mode_list** object outputs precisely the kind of list that we've been using so far to do our scale selection and mapping. Now, we're going to add an additional trick: the ability to transpose the scale/mode pattern chromatically.

To do this, we start with our pattern: each entry in the **coll** object represents the scale or mode pattern with respect to C natural. We're going to use the **zl rot** object to do our transposition by rotating (shifting to the right and wrapping around back to the beginning) our list the number of positions that correspond to our chromatic transposition (e.g. rotating 7 positions gives us the pattern for the selected scale/mode for G, rotating 10 positions gives us the pattern for the selected scale/mode for Bb, and so on).

The nice part of this modification is that – since we're still using our pattern of zeros and ones to specify our scales and modes – we can re-use the **scale_me** abstraction logic as is.

As before, there are keys and modes whose transformations result in more notes being output than others (try 1, 6, or 11). That result of combining numerical transposition with note filtering remains interesting, but wouldn't it be nice to be able to specify what happens to all those notes that are *not* played?

Arbitrary Scale Mapping

The third and final build-out of our simple sequencer provides an example of how we can perform arbitrary scale mapping for our sequenced output – the *03_transpose_mapper* patch.

Here's what our note-mapping sequencer looks like:

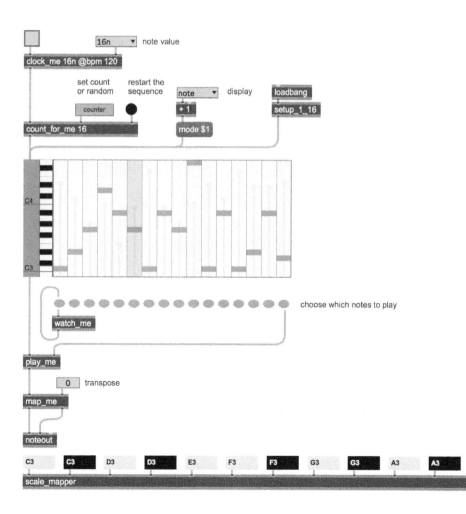

Quite a few parts of our initial simple sequencer are still there, but
the transposition abstraction portion of the patch – **map_me** – is
quite different. For one thing, we still have the very simple increment/
decrement patching from our old **transpose_me** abstraction, but we
now have a collection of twelve **number box** objects whose coloring and
arrangement strongly suggest the black and white keys on a keyboard.
You'll also notice that the **number boxes** are displaying MIDI notes by
pitch rather than as integer numbers.

They're all there to let us perform random keyboard mappings – we're
able to transpose any MIDI note number to (almost) any other MIDI note
number (the only exception will be those situations in which the MIDI
note numbers would transpose outside of the standard 0 – 127 MIDI note
number data range).

To see how the note mapping is done in this scale mapping patch, let's look inside the **scale_mapper** abstraction:

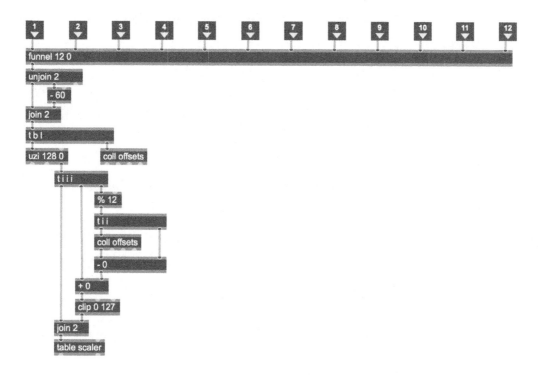

The patcher takes each of the twelve inputs – corresponding to twelve pitches – and uses the Max **funnel** object to create a two-item list for each input. For each note in the scale, the **funnel** object makes a list of the form *<pitch> <offset>*. The **coll offsets** object stores a table of scale offsets. After we've stored our table of offset values, the **uzi** object triggers a recalculation of the whole scale table any time an individual offset changes.

For each index in the 0 – 127 range:

- We use the **% 12** object to figure out which pitch (scale degree) we have and use that as an index to fetch the pitch offset from the **coll offsets** object.

- We add the original pitch and the offset (for the sake of hygiene, I've used a **clip** object to set min and max values to keep things in the normal MIDI note number 0 – 127 range).

- We finish the sequence for each note by using a **join** object to store the new scale values in the **table scaler**.

This maps the twelve input values we send to the **scale_mapper** abstraction across the *whole range* of the keyboard and provides us with a single **table** object we can use with output from the sequencer. And now that we're mapping all of the MIDI note numbers, this is all we need to do for transposition – no fancy filtering!

In the simplest case, all we really need to do is to fetch an incoming MIDI note from a list, add a transposition value, and use that number as an index into the **table** object, which will output the modified note for us on the fly. This means that the inside of the **map_me** abstraction is simple:

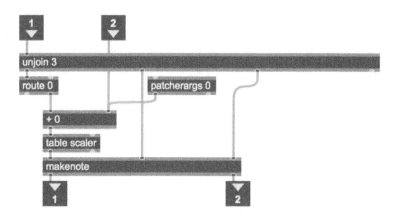

This mapping technique lets us map any note, regardless of whether it's in the scale or mode we're working in or not. We can create situations in which two different notes are mapped to the same output note and get rid of places where no note is played. The image below illustrates this feature – notice that both C natural and C# are mapped to C natural.

The **map_me** abstraction contains one more little hidden feature, implemented by the addition of a single Max object: the ability to *not play a note* with a given mapping. To do this, we chose a single MIDI note – it's the lowest MIDI note of all, but you could also use the highest note, since one is likely not to use either one in actual practice. The addition of a **route 0** object will pass any note which is not zero out the object's right outlet for transposition and scaling, and ignore any note number of zero. Since the Max **makenote** object only outputs a note pair when a value is received in its leftmost (i.e hot) inlet, no MIDI note messages will be sent, and the whole unpacking procedure will start anew when the next three-item list is sent to the **map_me** abstraction.

For our next chapter, we're going to do something sequencer-like – we're going to loop back to take another look at using the **live.step** object, and explore some of that object's further secrets.

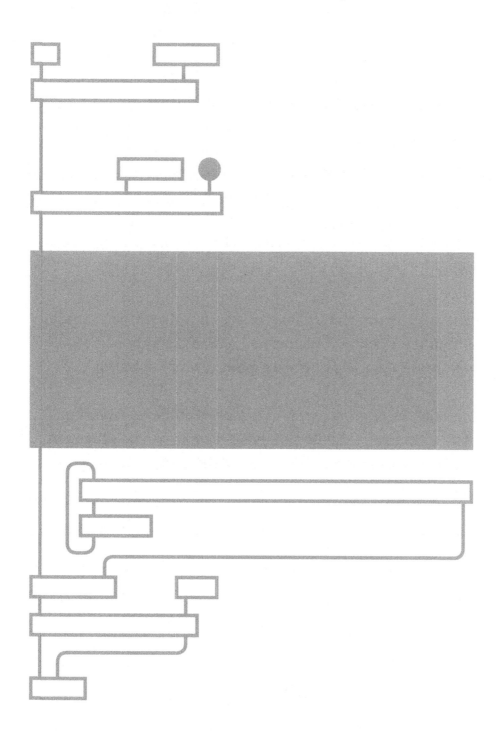

Creating step sequencers in Max is one of those tasks that tends to be pretty strongly affected by your own history of owning or using them – either as hardware or software. Ever since my first Korg SQ10, I've tended to think of sequences as ranks of sequences of 8 or 16 steps, and I've also tended to modify that idea in ways related to the physical box. For me, that's meant that I didn't automatically take to sequences that consisted of an odd numbers of steps as a single sequence with the number of steps that correspond to N times the number of steps (7, 14, 21 and so on) or a set of N subsequences of less than my trusty sixteen knobs' worth.

In the same way, I'm sure that there are those of you out there whose idea of a step sequencer is a Monome 64, 128, or 256. Or a Klee sequencer. Those visual and physical experiences are powerful.

For this tutorial, we're going to return to looking at the Max **live.step** object, but head off in a slightly different direction than polyphony or rotation. We're going to talk a little bit about managing sequences of different lengths and sizes, and working with units of time.

Forging The Chain

Our original consideration of the **live.step** object started with a very simple example of a counter-driven sequencer patch that included a group of sequences that were a uniform 16 steps in length.

We learned how to use messages to display and select which of those sequences we wanted to play back, and explored the enjoyable mayhem that ensues from turning everything on and then picking and choosing.

This time out, we're going to think of a collection of sequences in another way – as sequences that can be chained together to create longer sequences. And "longer" is the right word – the **live.step** object will store up to 16 sequences composed of up to 64 steps, giving us a single sequence of up to 1024 steps.

The *01_livestep_chaining* patch provides a small and simple example of how we can chain singles sequences together. As before our **live.step** object contains a set of four sequences, each having 16 steps, for a total of up to 64 events. The patch allows us to set monophonic playback of any number of steps (between 1 and 64). It displays the sequence, counts through it, and loops back when it hits the final step (which, as you'll recall, is numbered from 1 rather than 0).

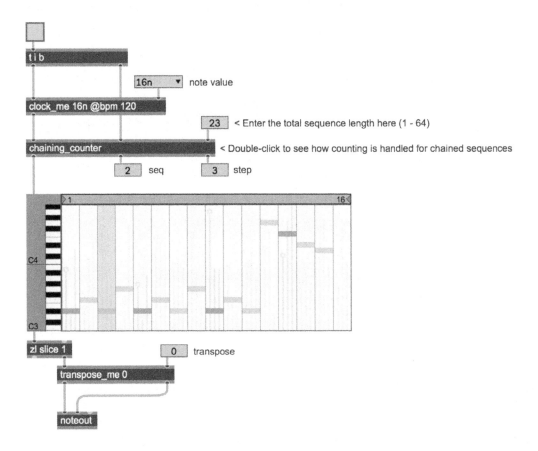

You'll recognize some of the contents of the the simple step sequencer patch such as the **clock_me** and the **transpose_me 0** abstractions and the **live.step** object. The main difference is the **chaining_counter** abstraction connected to the clock_me abstraction.

Let's take a look at the contents of the **chaining_counter** abstraction:

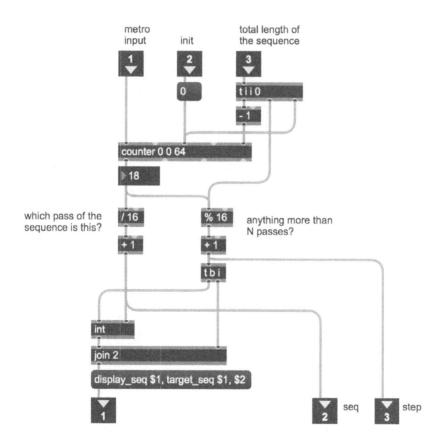

Managing the triggering of longer sequences is really a matter of counting – stepping through the proper number of steps while keeping in mind the length of the stored sequence.

Any given step will be identified by which of the sequences in the collection we're currently counting through, and which step in that sequence we're counting.

Once we get to the last item in a sequence, we send a message to change the target sequence we're working with, and wrap our count back to one. This abstraction adds two extra outlets so that you can watch the count in the parent patch.

Handling the user interface portion of the patch involves keeping track of which sequence in the stack we're currently counting through and then using the *target_seq* and *display_seq* messages to control what the **live.step** object displays.

The **chaining_counter** abstraction uses a **counter** object to set the length of the total count, a divide object (**/ 16**) to set the number of the sequence to trigger, and a remainder (**% 64**) object to choose the step in the sequence.

After that, it is simply a matter of sending a *target_seq* message to set the subsection of our larger sequence followed by a *display_seq* message to display the sequence visually, and an integer to specify the event in the current sequence we want to trigger.

With just a little modification and initialization, you can design sequences of any length from 1 to 1024 steps.

Keeping Things Odd

One of the interesting things about those early sequencers that captivated us is that – with very few exceptions – they all ran in cycles that were multiples of 8 or 16. Although it's not hard to figure out why that would have been the case, we can certainly imagine other cycle lengths. Now that we have a chaining counter, it's time to ask whether or not we can generalize the patching to cover other possibilities.

The **chaining_counter** abstraction suggests that there are two ways I can generalize things to serve odd-number sequence counting.

I can specify any number between 1 and 1024 for my total count. That means that I can think of it as N measures of an arbitrary number of steps (that is, 13 instead of the 16 in my example), where that arbitrary number of steps can be any number between 1 and 64.

That's where things start to get interesting – particularly if that number between 1 and 64 is the product of two other numbers. For example, 24 steps can be thought of as a sequence of 2 12-step units, 3 8-step units, 4 6-step units and or 6 4-step units, depending on how you want to divide them. Each collection of sequences could be thought of as different groupings.

The *livestep_chaining_2* patch makes a few simple modifications that give us more flexible playback.

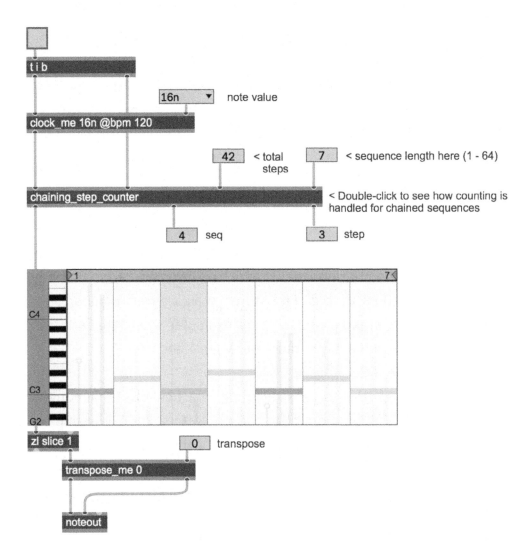

The contents of the **chaining_counter** abstraction differ surprisingly little from the original, considering the flexibility they provide (the changes made to the original patch are shown in the shaded areas).

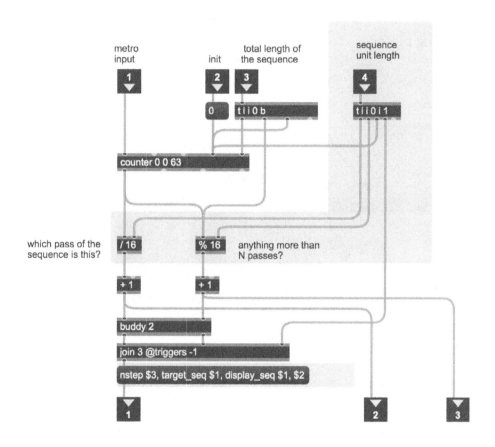

Not much to it, really – I added an **inlet** to set the sub-sequence length, meaning that our length of sequences can now be any number up to 64. In addition, I wanted the number of steps in a sequence as displayed by the **live.step** object to match my subsequence size, so I added the *nstep <# of steps in the sequence>* message when displaying a sequence as a part of the output of the patcher.

Right On Time

Wouldn't it be great to have my **live.step** sequence control and change
the rate at which the **metro** ran instead of having a straight and
unchanging pulse?

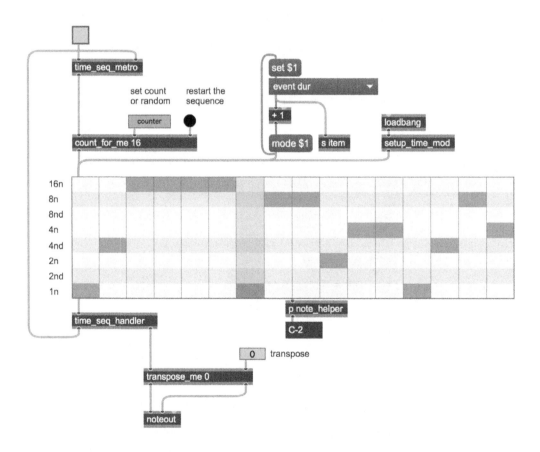

The example *03_livestep_time* patch provides an example of how we
might do that.

The starting point for this particular outing assumes a few things in the name of transparency and simplicity. First, I'm going to use Max's ITM features when it comes to implementing things that have to do with time. Once I do that, all I need to worry about is making sure that Max's Global Transport is running. I can refer to increments of time using the notevalue format for ITM objects (1n, 4nd, 8n, and so on). I can use those values to control a bunch of Max objects – most particularly, the **metro** object.

The *03_notevalue_metro* patch is a simple example of a patch whose metronome resets itself to ITM time values on the fly. In this case, I'm going to be using a subset of the available ITM note values:

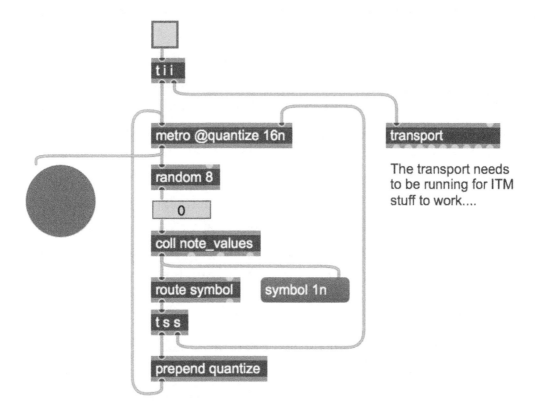

The transport needs to be running for ITM stuff to work....

We've got a **coll** (**coll note_values**) that stores the subset of note values
we want to work with, and use a **random** object to drive their selection.
With every tick of the **metro** object, we randomly grab a new unit of time
in note value format and use it to set the rate and quantization values for
the metronome.

Now that we have the outline of a patch that will allow us to reset
our **metro** object on the fly using the contents of a **coll**, it would be
useful to know how to use the **live.step** object to store that note value
information. A sequence would then let us specify the time durations
between one *bang* message sent from a **metro** object and the next one,
and change that duration while the sequence plays.

That means that the **live.step** object will need to store an additional value
besides its normal MIDI note number, velocity, and duration information.
The **live.step** object helpfully includes two additional and currently
unused parameters associated with each step of each sequence in our
collection of sequences – extra1 and extra2.

With the exception of the ranges we use for duration values, we've got
four values for each step in our sequence that we can set to the range
of 0 - 127. We're going to use one of those unused values – *extra1* – to
store MIDI note numbers (don't worry, we'll keep the note durations as
they are).

The **live.step** object has a useful user interface message that I can
repurpose to provide a way to display a small number of choices – the
fold message. The **live.step** object's fold mode (enabled/disabled by the

message *fold 1/0*) was initially created to let you choose to display all
possible available pitches or only a specific set of them (i.e. a scale or
mode), but you don't need to think of it that way. You can also think of
it as a way to specify a specific number of possible sequencing choices
for each step of the sequence and to use that subset as part of your
patching.

Setting the **live.step** object to display a subset of notes (which is what
we're using to specify the note values for our **metro** object) and to add
the *extra1* parameter takes a couple of messages to control folding, a
couple more to tweak the display so that it's more to my liking, and a
message to enable the *extra1* parameter output. That's done using the
setup_time_mod abstraction.

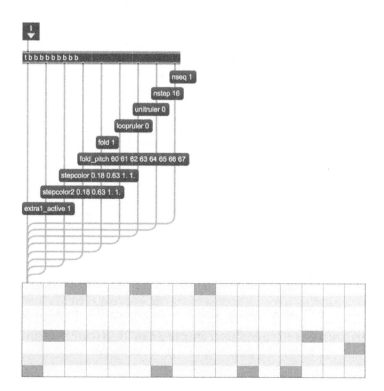

- We set the number of sequences and steps (one sequence of 16 steps, in this example) using the *nseq 1* and *nstep 16* messages.

- We don't want the note-based unit ruler any more since I'll be displaying options for timing rather than pitches. The message *unitruler 0* turns that off.

- We don't want to use the loop ruler either, so *loopruler 0* turns that off.

- The message *fold 1* enables the folding feature.

- We can set the specific range of pitch values to display (which we'll be using as placeholder for time values) with the message *fold_pitch 60 61 62 63 64 65 66 67*.

- The step colors in the UI assume pitch, so we'll set them all to the same color using the *stepcolor* and *stepcolor2* messages.

- To enable output for the extra1 parameter (which we're going to use to store the MIDI note number), we use the *extra1_active 1* message.

The result gives us a nice display that shows only the set of steps associated with the time values we want to use, and enables the extra1 parameter's output for use as a MIDI note number.

Let's turn our attention to using the output from the **live.step** object to generate MIDI note messages and modify our metronome on the fly.

The first thing we'll need to think about is that our normal **live.step** output is going to be working a little differently. The standard **live.step** output we've been working with throughout the tutorial so far has taken the form of a four-item list

1. The sequence event number

2. A MIDI note number

3. A velocity value

4. A duration value

This time, we're going to be using the MIDI note number as an index to grab note values to set the metronome on the fly. We need another value to use for the MIDI note number – that's why we enabled the *extra1* parameter. It has the same 0 - 127 parameter range we use for MIDI note numbers. As we've set up the **live.step** object, we're now getting a different list that looks like this:

1. The sequence event number

2. An index for time values

3. A velocity value

4. A duration value

5. A MIDI note number (the *extra1* value)

The biggest difference has to do with how we format our MIDI note messages now, and the **time_seq_handler** abstraction demonstrates how we do that:

We need to do a little simple message rearrangement – we'll still be stripping off the sequence event number and using the remainder of the list to do two things:

1. We use the second item in our list to index a **coll** object and fetch the time value we'll send to our **metro** object. A simple **message** box using the *$* substitution (*$2*) will do that.

2. The third, fourth, and fifth items are used to construct our MIDI note message, but they're out of order – the MIDI note number (*extra1*) is the last item on the list, but we need to use it as the first item in our note number/velocity/duration MIDI message. Once again, we can use *$* substitutions (*$5 $3 $4*) in a **message** box to rearrange the three items in our list and output them as a new MIDI note message list. The resulting list is sent to the **makenote** object in the **transpose_me** abstraction downstream in the parent patch.

As you would imagine, the *03_livestep_time* patch requires an interaction between the output of the **live.step** object and the part of the patch that serves as the metronome. As we saw, the **time_seq_handler** abstraction sends a new note value for each step in the sequencer, which we connect to the second inlet of the patcher that serves as our metronome: the **time_seq_metro** abstraction. This patcher takes our earlier *ITM_metro* patcher and uses it to control a **metro** object.

Here's what's inside the **time_seq_metro** abstraction:

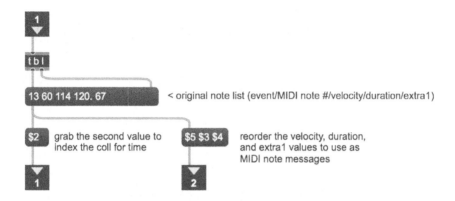

The left inlet turns the **metro** object on and off, and also turns the Global Transport on and off as well – we need the Global Transport to be on any time we're working with note values.

The right inlet takes the time value from the **time_seq_handler** abstraction and uses it to set the new time value for the **metro** object. We set up our **live.step** object to have 8 possible output values to specify the time. The **coll ITM_values** object receives a value from the **time_seq_handler** abstraction and uses that as an index to fetch a note value to set the **metro** object. We use the same set of numbers for indices (60-67) that we used when setting up the *fold_pitch* message for the **live.step** object.

The *livestep_time* patch contains a couple of other features I added to make working with the patch a little easier. First, I added a **umenu** object whose menu items were set using the object's Inspector in a way that made it easier to navigate the **live.step** object for editing – when you choose a menu item, the mode message changes the **live.step** object's display.

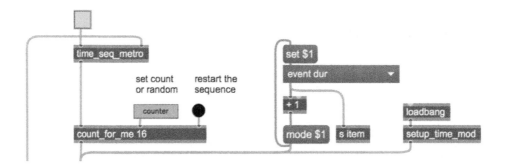

Since the output of the *extra1* parameter is an integer in the range of 0 – 127, I'd really like to be able to see what MIDI pitch the extra1 parameter is set to instead of seeing just the slider. To do that, I added the **note_ helper** abstraction. When the **umenu** is set to display pitch, the patcher displays MIDI pitches when you move a slider.

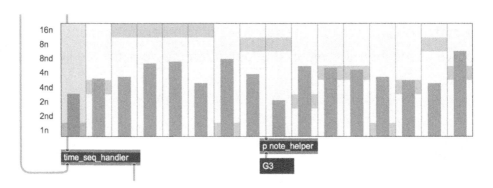

The inside of the **note_helper** abstraction is pretty simple. Whenever I select a menu item for displaying **live.step** settings in the parent patch, the menu item number is sent to the **note_helper** abstraction. If the menu item number matches the *extra1* parameter (3), then the slider values are passed through the patcher to a Max integer **number box** that I've set up to display MIDI pitch values.

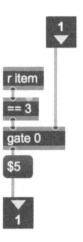

So there you have it – a nice **live.step**-based bit of patching that implements a slightly more interesting step sequence. That's it for this chapter. In a future chapter, we'll be looking at a completely different way to access the contents of your **live.step** object.

For now, it's time to execute another loopback and investigate just how it is that our step sequencer keeps time.

Beating Time

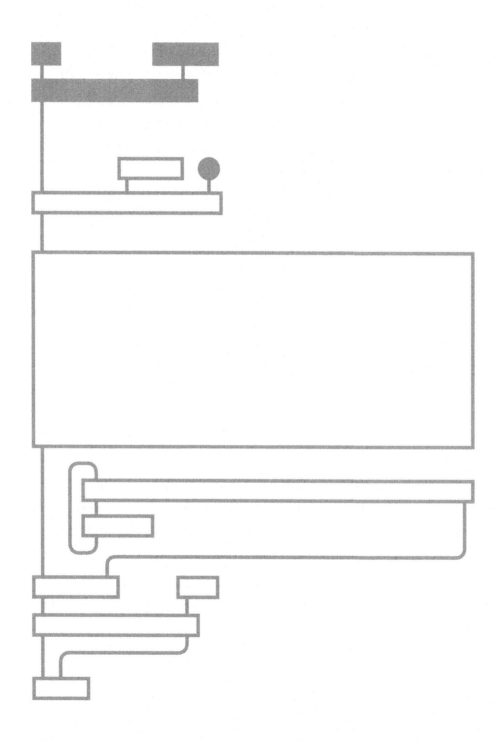

This sequence of chapters has proceeded to examine individual functional parts of our original step sequencer patch, and taken each of them as starting points for adding new features or rethinking the ideas behind those functional parts. Now, it's time to think about... well, *time*.

Up at the very top of our simple step sequencer patch, we have a Max **clock_me** abstraction that produces the bang messages that drive the **count_for_me** abstraction that steps through the MIDI note messages stored in the **live.step** object.

In our simple sequencer patch, the **clock_me** abstraction takes advantage of the ability to specify units of time to Max objects in ways that make more sense to musicians. At one time, the **metro** object only worked with values in milliseconds. Anyone who wanted to set the rate of a **metro** object had to calculate the relationship between tempo and millisecond values, and then decide what unit of musical time they wanted the **metro** object to output its bang messages at (quarter note, eighth note, etc.).

Max now lets you use a master clock to keep track of time by means of the **transport** object. In addition to having a single point of control for things in your Max patch, the **transport** object allows you to specify time in terms of musical note values (the transport needs to be running for this to work, as we pointed out in the first chapter) – our **metro** object in the original simple sequencer patch lets us select the musical intervals we want to output sequencer events at by sending messages to the **metro** object's right inlet from a **live.menu** object.

There are a number of other Max objects that also understand that same way of referring to time – the Max delay object, MSP objects such as the **phasor~** object, and even the **makenote** object that we use to create sets of note-on and note-off messages in our step sequencer.

The messages related to note values are very useful but you've probably noticed that they're limited to note values (e.g. 4n for a quarter note), their dotted equivalents (e.g. 4nd), and triplets (e.g. 4nt). The world is full of musicians who want more than triplets, and musical traditions whose polyrhythms are more exotic than 3-against-2 or 4-against-3. How can we modify our sequencer to work with subdivisions of note values that are not in threes (n-tuplets)?

Dividing Your Time: phasor~ and rate~

One of the interesting features of using the **metro** object with note values is that we're specifying the length of time between *bang* messages for the **metro** object rather than saying anything about when the **metro** object is turned on. This is kind of a subtle distinction that produces interesting results. You can create a patch that contains a number of **metro** objects that all have the same argument for their rate (say, *4n*) and then start each of the **metro** objects at different times – the result won't be synchronized, although each individual **metro** object will wait exactly the duration of a quarter note between the *bang* messages it sends out.

You can synchronize a number of **metro** objects to be in sync with the transport's master clock by telling each of them to start when the transport object is turned on. To do this, we use the attribute *@active 1* and specify how output is quantized using the attribute *@quantize* followed by a time value (*8n*, for example).

These attributes are very useful in situations where you might want to have two **live.step** objects being driven by two **metro** objects running at different note value rates. When you start up the **transport** object, any **metro** object in any patch with the *active* attribute set to one will start counting.

But what about increments of time that don't easily correspond to more traditional note values?

In simplest terms, the note values that Max knows about if you use a
transport object are subdivisions of a whole note (1n) divided by units of
2 (2n) or 3 (1nt). As we go, in turn, to subdivisions of that note, we just
divide by 2 all the way down, and dotted note values are one-and-a-half
times any of our normal note values. To create a general **metro**-like patch
that outputs other integer subdivisions than 2 or 3, we can move into
the MSP world of audio-rate triggering, which is simple to use, and very
accurate. Here's how it works.

Just as the Max **metro** object lets us specify a time duration, there's an
MSP object that lets us create a function that ramps from a value of 0.
to a value of 1.0 using those same time units: the MSP *phasor~* object.
While the *phasor~* object normally takes an argument that specifies a
frequency in Hertz, it also works with the same note values, as long as
there is a Max transport object running. In addition, you can also "lock"
the rate at which your function's output ramps from 0. to 1.0 in relation
to the **transport** (using the *@lock 1* attribute).

Moreover, if you're working in Max for Live, the Live application's
transport is used as the master clock for your Max patches.

But there's a problem: the **phasor~** object outputs waveforms rather
than Max events. How can we turn a **phasor~** object's output to a
sequence of bang messages?

To do that, we make use of a trio of MSP objects that work at signal rate: a **delta~**, **←0.5~** and **edge~** object. Connecting these three objects to the output of a **phasor~** object will provide us with a *bang* message at the rate that the **phasor~** object runs:

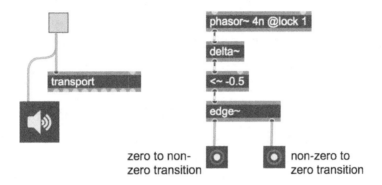

The tempo from which the note values are derived can be set by sending the message *tempo <bpm>* to the **transport** object. If you're working in Max for Live, the tempo is set using the Live application itself.

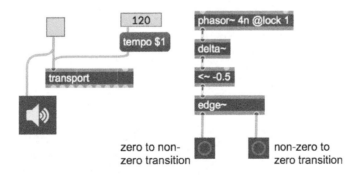

Now that we have a reliable way to convert **phasor~** output to *bang* messages we can use with our step sequencer, it's time to reflect on what advantages that might have for us.

Up until this point, we've found the use of the **metro** object along with the **transport** object to be a great advantage in terms of letting us specify units of time as the note values we're used to working with. As useful as that is, it's not really possible to easily work outside of that system – either values that are not halves or triplets of a note value, or time scales that are longer than a single measure (*1n*). Given our new **delta~/<~/edge~** Max trick, there's an MSP object that will let us do just that: the **rate~** object.

The **rate~** object lets you time-scale the output of a **phasor~** object – it takes the output of a **phasor~** object as its input, and then time-scales the output based on a multiplier value you give it in the form of an argument or a message to the **rate~** object's right inlet. If you give it a number less than 1.0, you'll generate several ramps for each cycle of the main **phasor~** object. Numbers greater than 1.0 will produce ramps that take longer to cycle than the original **phasor~** itself.

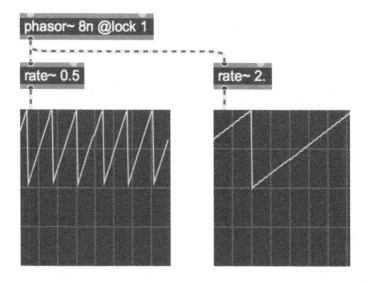

By cleverly combining **phasor~** and **rate~** objects together with the **delta~/<~/edge~** objects, you can create all kinds of interesting ways to create *bang* messages to drive your sequencer, and the great advantage is that any **rate~** objects you use will be driven in sync with the **phasor~** object they're connected to. Do you want a really slow sequencer that outputs a note once every 4 bars? Grab a **phasor~** object and set it as **phasor~ 1n @lock 1**, send its output to a **rate~ 4.** object, and then use the **delta~, ←0.5~** and **edge~** objects to output the *bang* message to drive your sequencer. Would you like to drive two **live.step** objects in sync with an arbitrary multiple? The same technique works well.

N-tuplets

The trick to producing n-tuplets as a way to drive your step sequencer follows on nicely from the technique we've just described – it has to do with having a reliable way to generate *N* beats per unit of time and doing so in a way that's accurate. The **rate~** object was created to do just that.

The *01_beating_time_1* example patch lets you specify n-tuplet outputs for any of the standard note values.

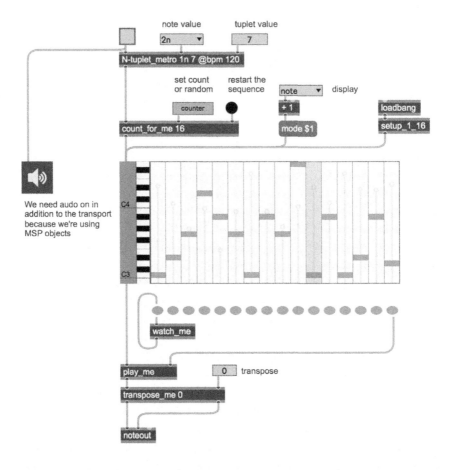

To see how it works, double-click on the **N-tuplet_metro** abstraction to look inside:

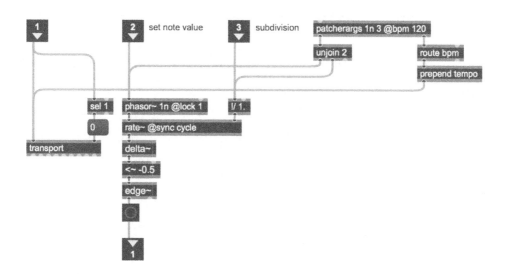

As we did with our simple step sequencer, We're controlling the **transport** object with an external toggle and resetting the transport (the first inlet). We're using note values to set the rate of our events (the second inlet). In this case, we're setting the length of a **phasor~** object's sweep rather than the time between ticks of a **metro** object. To derive the n-tuplet, we simply time scale that output by setting a **rate~** object. An easy way to derive the **rate~** object's value is to use a **/!** object with an argument of *1.0* (the third inlet), which calculates the reciprocals of whole number value (e.g. a value of 3 will set the **rate~** object's time-scaling to .333, which will output triplets). Adding the **delta~, <~ -0.5** and **edge~** objects from before, we transform the waveform output into *bang* messages.

While you'll recognize the use of the **patcherargs** object to initialize
values and let us use arguments and attributes, there's something a little
different this time around – we have two arguments instead of just one
(**N-tuplet_metro 1n 7**) in addition to our normal attribute.

If the **patcherargs** object has more than one argument, it will output a
message consisting of the values associated with each argument (note
that – like regular Max arguments – they need to be typed in order!). To
grab both arguments, we add an **unjoin 2** object and then connect the
outputs to the places the data is needed. That's all there is to it.

Polyrhythms

The *02_beating_time_2* example patch is a little more exotic – rather than specifying an equally-spaced set of *bang* messages, you can specify a polyrhythm that generates two different subdivisions of a single time interval for 3-against-2 or 5-against-8 rhythms.

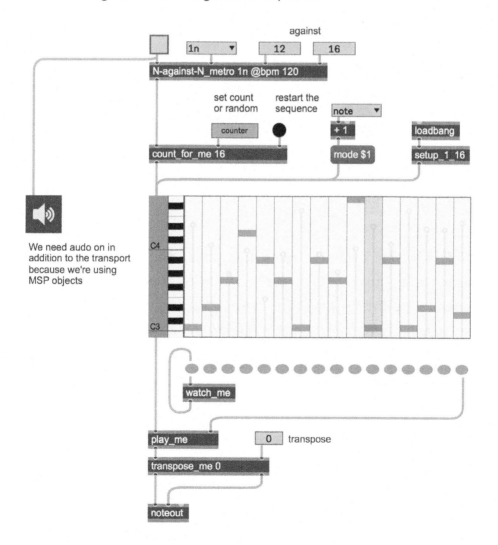

Double-click on the **N-against-N_metro** abstraction to see how it's done:

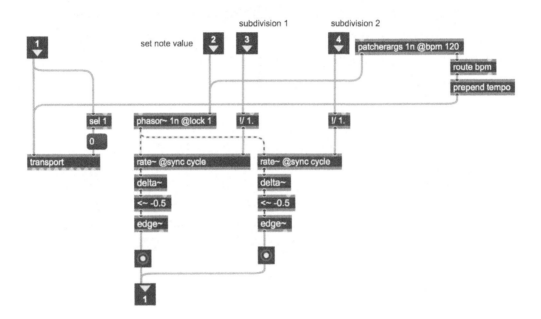

As before, we start with the same note values, and then use the single **phasor~** object to drive two **rate~** objects in series, each of which has a separate subdivision value. The **rate~** object can generate all kinds of interesting patterns that – once you know the little trick for generating *bangs* from **rate~/phasor~** output – can create all kinds of interesting skewed triggering schemes.

Finally, why limit yourself to driving a single sequence? The *beating_ time_3* patch repurposes the **N-against-N_metro** abstraction by separating out the two outputs and driving two sequences separately.

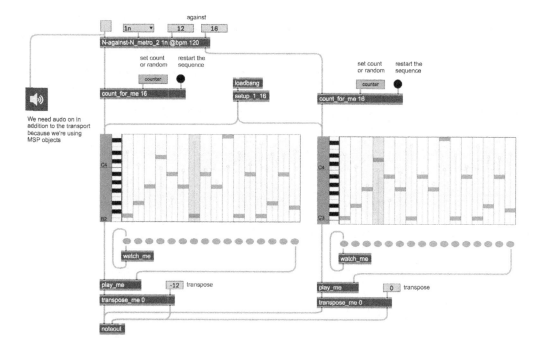

The only difference between the **N-against-N_metro** and **N-against-N_metro_2** abstractions is the separation of the two **rate~** objects' outputs. It's that simple.

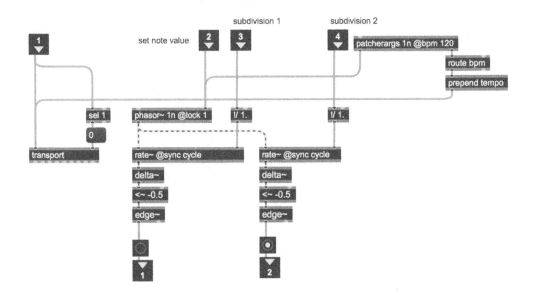

As long as we're thinking about timing, we'll turn our attention back again to the idea of silence as a kind of timed event, and think and explore a bit more about playing/not playing.

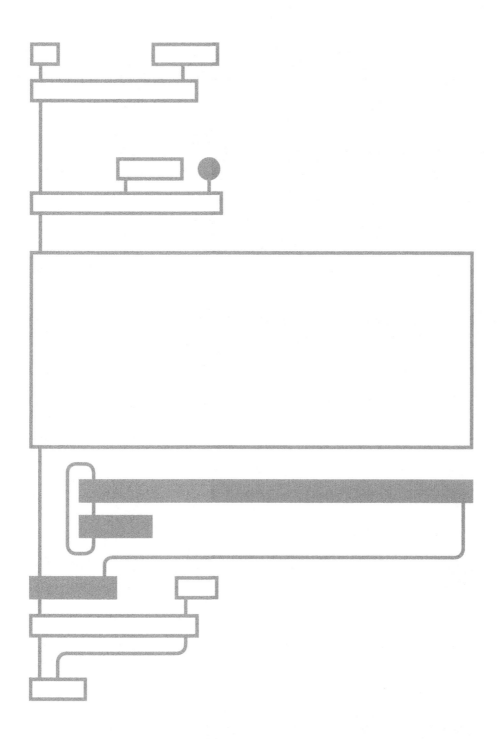

When you think about it, the balance of silence and activity in music exists on a number of different time scales – particularly in ensemble situations. In addition to the choices a player makes to play or not play, there's also the larger set of patterns that emerge when performing in the same space as others – are players "soloing?" Are they working off the same material and adding their own variations in real time based on a shared set of materials? Do we think of what we hear as vertical or horizontal collections or variations of note events?

Those are questions that occur in all kinds of musical cultures. When we start thinking about step sequencer output in terms of these ideas, some interesting things begin to happen – we begin to think of sequences in terms of density over spans of time rather than what happens when the next event occurs. In this chapter, we're going to explore this idea a bit.

Event Density (the drunkard's walk)

In our last investigation of playing/not playing we created a patcher called **%_gate 50** for use in the *random_percentage_sequencer* example patch that worked probabilistically. Every time it received a list of MIDI note values (event number, MIDI note number, velocity, duration), the patcher generated a random number that was tested against a settable percentage value. If the value was less than or equal to the percentage value, the MIDI note values were passed through to be played.

That patch worked well, but it always remains trapped in an eternal present: the patch deals only with what happens when the next event occurs. Wouldn't it be more interesting to find a way of modifying the percent probability in a more subtle way?

For our next example patch, we're going to replace the **%_gate 50** abstraction with some new patching using an object we haven't used so far: the **drunk** object.

The **drunk** object takes its name from the a famous stochastic process called a "drunkard's walk." Rather than generating a new random number with each iteration that falls in a given range, the drunkard's walk begins with a value and then lets us specify the range within which the next output will deviate, up or down. The "next step" will be a random number that falls within the specified range which is then added to the previous output value, so changing the range for that next step has very different outcomes. Very low step values produce output that meanders about, very high step values look and act very much like ordinary random number outputs, and medium values produce something in between.

This is easier to see than to explain, and the *drunk_test_1* patch will let you experiment with different values.

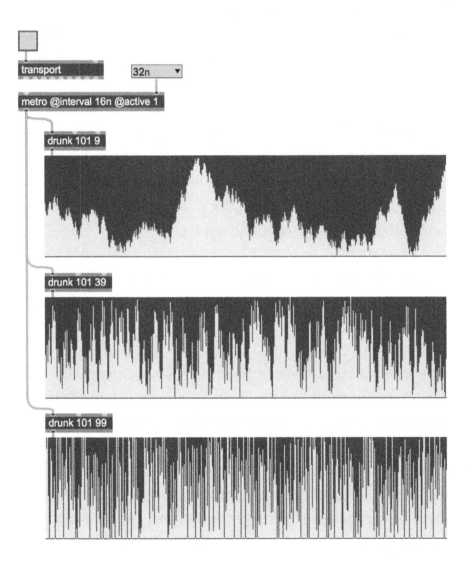

Now that we've seen the **drunk** object in action, let's use it to create a new patcher that combines this feature with the percentage testing we've already created for our **%_gate** abstraction – the **drunk_gate** abstraction. Here's what's inside:

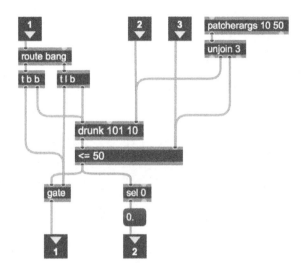

The **drunk_gate** abstraction replaces the **random 101** object used in the **%_gate** abstraction with a **drunk 101 10** object, and adds an inlet to set the step size the **drunk** object will use when it generates its next random value.

Since we now have two parameters we'd like to set using the **patcherargs** object, need to modify the patch slightly. When the **patcherargs** object uses more than one argument, it sends three values from its left outlet – the name of the patcher itself, followed by the two values in order. We use an **unjoin** object to grab the initial values for the step and the percentage value against which the **drunk** output is tested. We send those values to the **drunk** and **<=** objects respectively.

The *drunk_test_2* patch will let you experiment with different settings for the step and percentage range values.

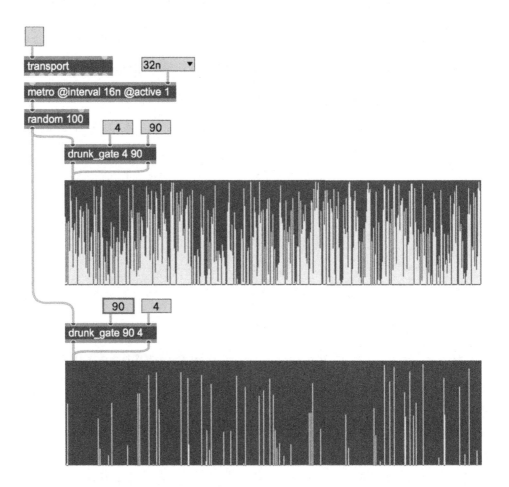

The *01_drunken_sequencer* patch adds the **drunk_gate** abstraction as part of our basic sequencer.

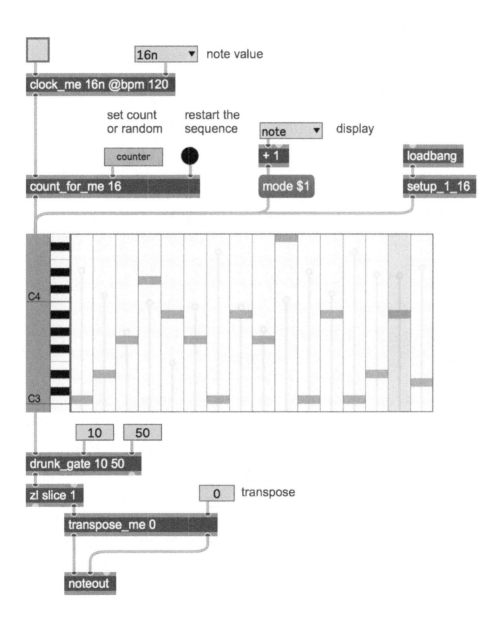

An interesting minor variation, shown in the *02_drunken_sequencer_2*
patch, lets you hear what happens when you drive the same sequence
with two **drunk_gate** abstractions – stochastic unisons. Remember,
keeping an eye out for minor variations can produce intriguing results.

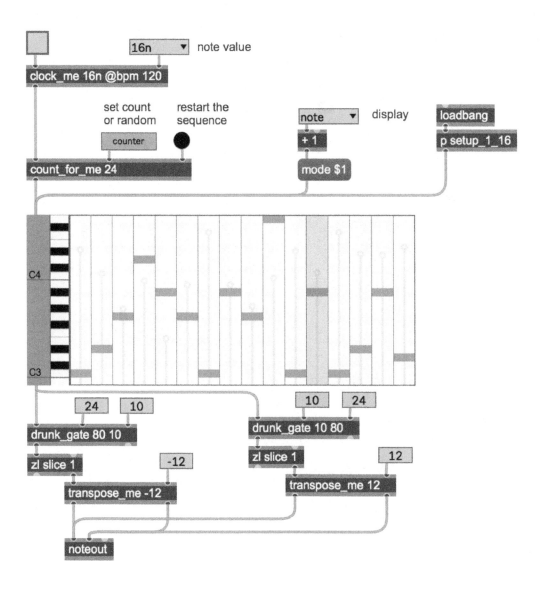

Location Location Location (Once Again)

As we saw in the previous tutorial about playing/not playing, we can look once again at the assumption we've made about the ordering of data that flows from one functional unit of the patch to another.

The *location_location_2* patch uses the **drunk_gate** abstraction in two different places in our simple sequencer, with two very different effects: Two variations of the playback for two sequences.

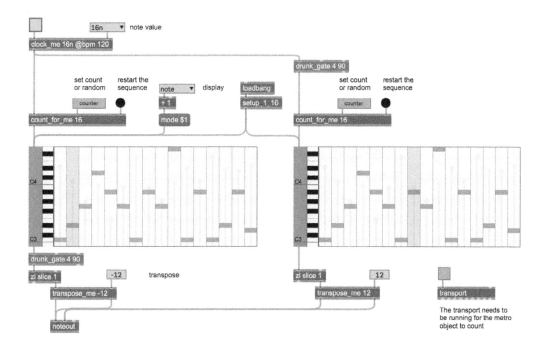

As before, the **clock_me** abstraction is driving what is essentially two versions of the very same patch. In the left version of the sequencer, the **drunk_gate** abstraction is sitting where we initially placed it, making a probabilistic decision whether to pass the list on or not whenever a new list of numbers arrives.

The right portion of the patcher differs again in that the **drunk_gate** abstraction is located between the **metro** object and the **count_for_me** abstraction. When the patcher is used at the top of the sequencer patch, the probabilistic output will determine whether a *bang* message is sent to the **count_for_me** abstraction – the result being that the sequencer doesn't "skip a step" when the **metro** sends a **bang** message. Sometimes, however, it waits to play the next step .

When the patcher is used farther down in the sequencer, the probabilistic output will determine whether or not a step in the sequence will be "skipped" or not. As before, the step sequencers on the right are transposed to make their output more easily audible.

To Play Or Not To Play (Euclidean version)

Another of the interesting modifications to our simple sequencer may seem somewhat unrelated to the discussion of playing/not playing sequencer events that we've had so far: the Euclidean sequencer.

Generally speaking, Euclidean sequencers concern themselves with fitting or distributing a certain number of events as equally as possible within a defined parameter – an approach you can apply to anything that involves triggering events in time.

The technique is as easily applied to sequences as it is to rhythms, where we think primarily of the triggering of the same event over and over (a kick drum or another sample). After all, what we're really talking about is a group of event triggers associated with another group of musical note events.

In the course of our tutorial on step sequencing, we have already done
most of the patching we need to make a Euclidean sequencer of our
own. Are you surprised? Maybe that's because all of the user interfaces
we're shown for Euclidean sequencers tend to be overwhelmingly visual,
and based around the notion of events arranged in a circle. Here's an
example: The beautiful and elegant Rhythm Necklace app for iPhones
and iPads:

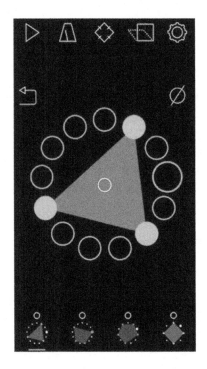

The problem with this practice is that anyone who wants to explore
making their own Euclidean sequencer will probably start by trying to
create those circular graphics. I think it's simpler to think of Euclidean
sequencing not as a circle, but as a cycle. And our basic step sequencer
already has an example of events in a cycle.

It's right there in our basic step sequencer below the **live.step** object:

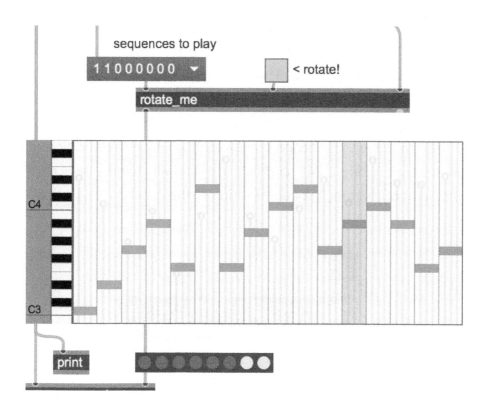

Lots of Euclidean sequencers seem to be fond of sequences composed of numbers that are simultaneously divisible by 2 and 3 (8, 12, 24, 36, 48, etc.) because they simplify the idea of working with 3 against 2 polyrhythms. We're going to start there with a simple example, and then add an additional feature or two.

When dealing with sequences longer than 16 steps, we'll need to make a
change to our setup abstraction. By default, the **live.step** object displays
16 steps, which has been fine for our example patches. But there's
something else you haven't seen – there's also a default loop setting
that the **live.step** object uses. That default loop setting isn't something
we're actually using at all, but it's also something that isn't changed
automatically when you set a sequence step length of longer than 16 –
we'll need to make that change ourselves. It will take the addition of a
single message – *loop 1 24* – and nothing else will change. We'll add it to
the inside of our **setup_1_24** abstraction in the patches in this chapter.

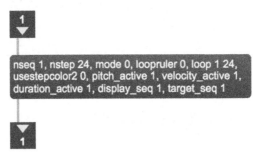

Dealing With Distribution

We've already got the patching necessary to play sequences back, and also what we need to turn out sequences on and off. The only thing we really need is a way to distribute a given number of events as evenly as possible across a given number of possible outputs.

The patch *04_euclidean_1* contains an example of how we might do that.

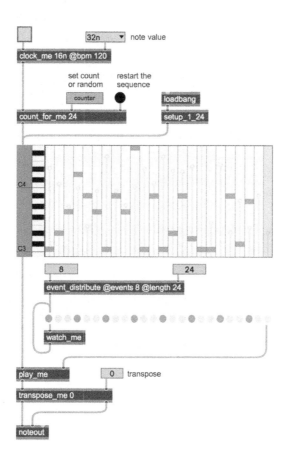

This patch looks a lot like the basic step sequencer patch, with
a few changes:

- We have added a new bit of patching – the **event_distribute @events
  8 @length 24** abstraction.

- We are using the **setup_1_24** abstraction to do some setup for the
  live.step object's appearance,

- We are using a different argument to the **count_for_me** abstraction
  to set its upper range

- We are modifying the **matrixctrl** object using its Inspector to support
  24 steps.

The work of doing the event distribution happens inside the **event_ distribute @events 8 @length 24** abstraction:

The inside of the patch is yet another testimonial to the usefulness of the **trigger** object. When we set the number of items we want to distribute, a **trigger** object (**t b i i clear**) clears the **matrixctrl** object's display, sets the number of events we want to use for calculation, and triggers the calculation. When we set the length of our list of events, a second **trigger** object (**t i i**) resets the number of columns the **matrixctrl** object displays, resets the length of our output list, and triggers the calculation. Once the pattern for the **matrixctrl** object is sent out, it's converted to a list of ones and zeros with the help of the **watch_me** abstraction, as before.

And again, we're using a **patcherargs** object to treat the length of our sequence and the number of events to distribute as attributes (*@events* and *@length*, respectively). I decided to use attributes here because attributes can be typed in in any order. I wasn't sure I'd be able to remember which argument came first.

Adding the **event_distribute @events 8 @length 24** abstraction means that we can start thinking of our patch as a way to trigger those events in a given sequence that corresponds to their distribution across the whole 24 steps. For example, the resulting sequences will have something in common if the *@events* attributes of two of them are multiples of one another.

The *05_euclidean_2* patch contains an example of what happens when
we trigger the same sequence in order and then use two instances of the
distribution patcher that are set to different numbers of events:

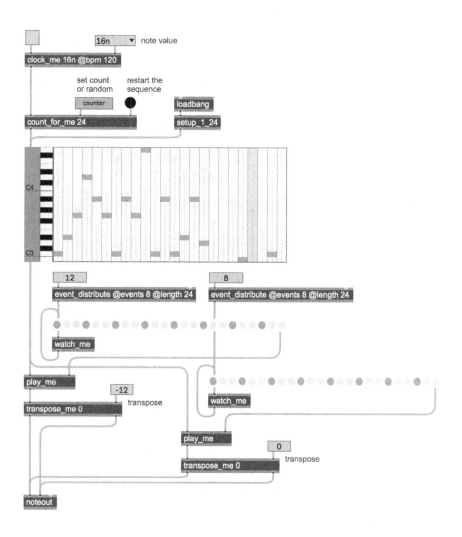

The result will be polyrhythm as an output (12 against 8) that shares the
same set of sequencer events (both outputs have been transposed so
that you can hear the difference).

Location Location Location (One More Time)

If you're listening carefully, you've noticed by now that our Euclidean sequencer is actually choosing which events in a sequence to play once it has determined its distribution.

What about creating a patch whose event triggering (rather than the events it plays) is distributed – one where the full sequence is played back at a rhythm specified by that same distribution of events?

It turns out that we can make a minor change to the distribution patcher and the original **matrixctrl/watch_me/play_me** patching we already have in order to add a way to do just that to the metronome portion of our patch. The *euclidean_metro* patch demonstrates what the change looks like:

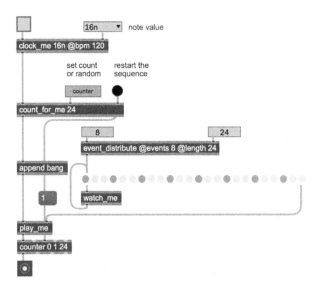

We took the original **matrixctrl/p watch_me/p play_me** patching we already had and moved it earlier in the patch, so that it stepping through the list of distributed events was done using the original **count_for_me** abstraction driven by the **clock_me** abstraction.

The **play_me** abstraction in its original form took an input list and then passed or rejected that input based on the pattern sent by means of the **matrixctrl** object. All we did to set things up was to append a *bang* message to the count using the **append bang** object. The patching we copied works just as it did before, but this time it either passes a bang message or it doesn't. In turn, we're using that *bang* message to increment a second **counter** that counts through the **live.step** events (and is initialized when we restart the sequence). The result is a patch that outputs a set of distributed bangs – which can then be used to step through the events in the **live.step** object as normal.

The *06_euclidean_3* patcher folds this control scheme into our step
sequencer:

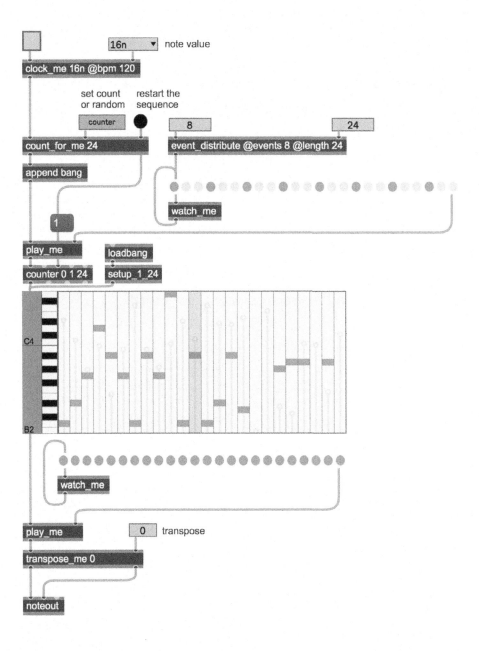

As before, you may wonder about the results of having two *euclidean_ metro* patches accessing the same sequence. The patcher *07_ euclidean_4* will let you explore the results for yourself.

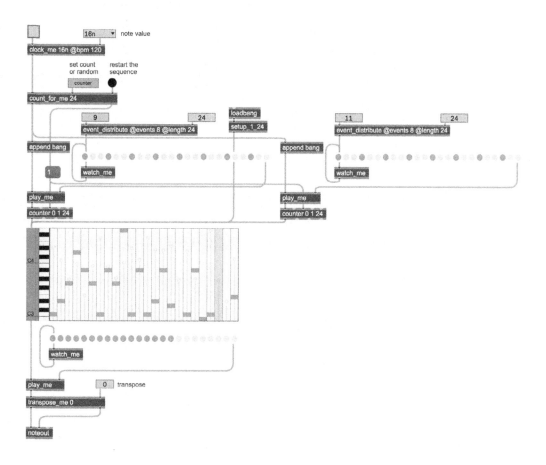

Heavy Rotation

In addition to the ability to distribute *N* events somewhat evenly across
a total number of events as a way of generating variety in rhythmic
patterns, Euclidean sequencers often generate further rhythmic variety
by "rotating" their patterns – a fascinating way to create new patterns or
produce surprising new results with a simple change. The patching we've
done in this book already contains the raw materials for us to do that
with our Euclidean sequences, too.

Let's go all the way back to the very first chapter in this book on using
the **live.step** object, where we created a patch that let us play any (or all)
of a collection of sequences by specifying a pattern of them, and then
"rotating" the pattern we chose.

Here's what the relevant part of the original patching looked like:

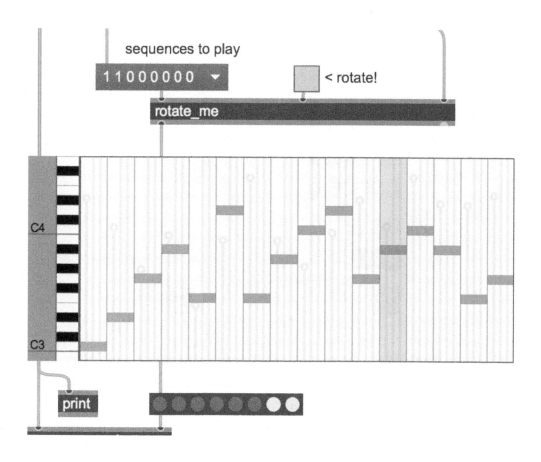

The **rotate_me** abstraction is what we're specifically interested in. Here are its original contents:

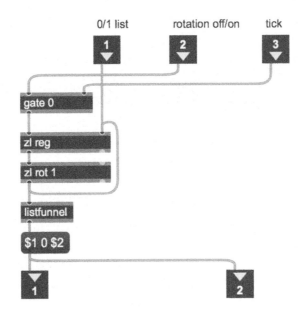

This patch accepted a list of zeros and ones as its input, and then triggered a forward rotation of the list each time it received a bang message. The combination of the **listfunnel** object and the *$1 0 $2* **message** box sent the resulting rotated pattern out of an outlet to a **matrixctrl** object.

Here's a variant of that same abstraction – eurotate_me that we can use with our Euclidean sequencer:

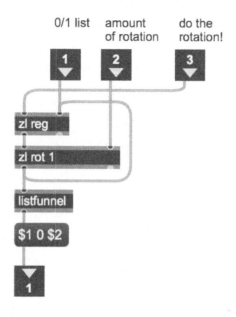

The changes are minimal – we lost the on/off gate logic, and instead added an inlet that let us rotate any input list by a number other than one (negative numbers rotate the list backward, of course).

The *08_euclidean_5* patch folds the new patching (in the form of the
eurotate_me abstraction) into our Euclidean rhythm generator:

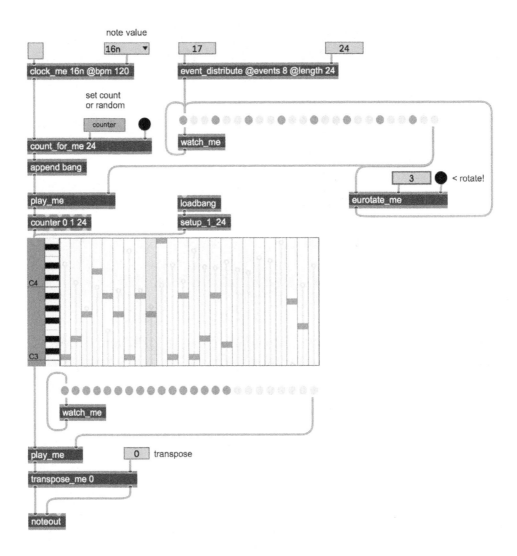

Of course, you can re-use the same patching logic on the lower part of
the sequencer patch to rotate which notes in a sequence will be played
back in distributed form, as in the *09_euclidean_6* patch.

It is the equivalent of having an "offset" in your sequence playback.

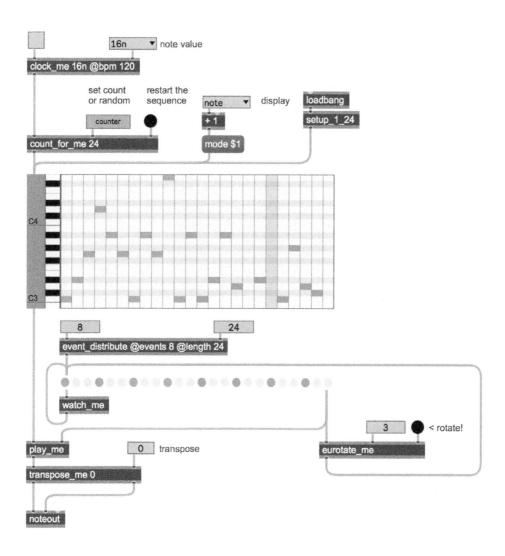

That sequence in the **live.step** object is now hiding and revealing itself in some really interesting ways. In our next chapter, we're going to loop back again to reveal some of the **live.step** object's other abilities.

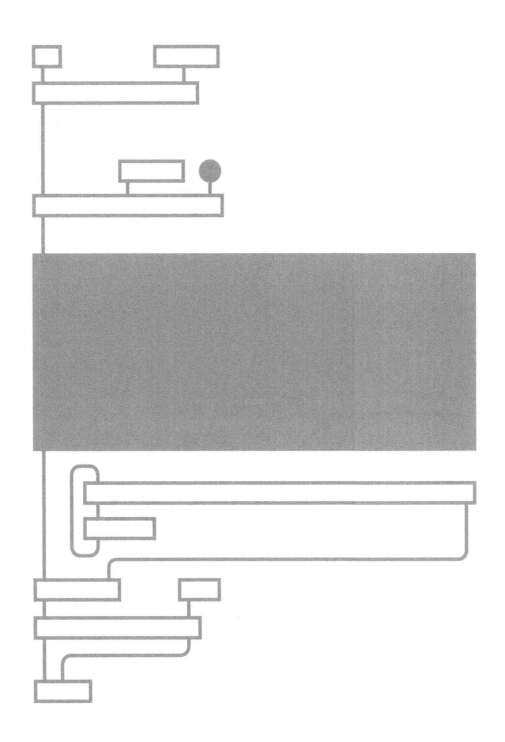

As interesting and enjoyable as it is, there are a few things about the **live. step** object that present themselves as constraints.

Often, we innovate when faced with constraints. It can be that satisfying moment when you realize that you do know a way around the problem you're facing. In other cases, it can be the sudden realization that what seems to be a problem is actually an interesting feature that redirects your original thinking.

In my experience, this is particularly true in the Max world – it seems as though each of the ways you could reach a goal offers its own particular opportunities for going a different way, or finding the interesting workaround. The very first chapter in this book contains an example of precisely that idea (finding an interesting workaround to the idea that the **live.step** object outputs either all of its stored data for every step in the stack of sequences, or only one at a time).

Working with chained sequences in our last tutorial may have given you some ideas, even if you weren't excited about arbitrarily long sequences with stacks of odd-numbered lengths. For example, how might one go about constructing step sequencer events by choosing the data that makes up the basic note-velocity-duration message from step values in *different* sequences in a **live.step** object that contained more than a single sequence?

You can, of course, set up a sequence of *target_seq* messages, fire 'em off, and then use the results to create your note event. You could even ask for a specific step in the sequence by queueing two messages

– a *target_seq* message to choose the target, followed by an integer to specify the step, collecting the result, and then continuing.

In this tutorial, we're going to take a little step sideways by talking about another way to do this – one that offers a wealth of interesting possibilities: using a Max dictionary as a way to work with the **live.step** object.

In a way, what this means is that you can use the **live.step** object to quickly and intuitively edit your sequences, dump the data into your dictionary, and then easily access all of the data for all of the steps for all of the sequences with a simple message with a very standard format.

Sequence to Dictionary – Fill 'er Up

You really should investigate the **live.step** object by spending a little time with the help files – it's an amazing Max object. I, myself, am only beginning to explore this subtle and deep object's capabilities. In the course of my own investigations, I noted that the object had a *dumpout* outlet (the third outlet). I discovered that this object can work with Max's dictionary data storage objects, and wondered what I could do with *that*.

The subject of creating and using dictionaries in Max is another of those places where the depth and options available to you might seem daunting or impenetrable. There are tutorial videos that demonstrate the **dict** object's uses, along with the helper objects that work with it that I commend to your attention. This time out, we're going to be keeping things really simple, since we don't *need* a lot to do a lot.

So let's start at the beginning: What's the dumpout outlet for, anyway? To investigate that, we can open the **live.step** object's help file, navigate to the "Filling and dumping data" tab, copy the contents to our clipboard, paste them into a new patcher, and then get rid of all the stuff we don't need. Lock the patch, and then click on the dump message with the Max window open and see what you get:

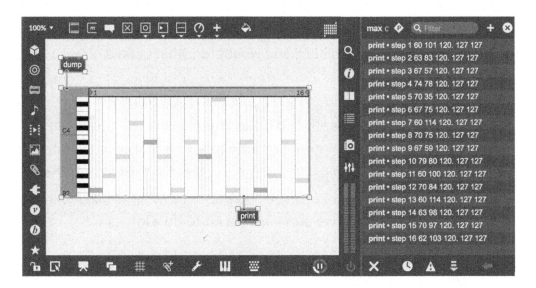

As you can see, sending the message *dump* to the **live.step** object will send everything out the dumpout outlet in a specific and regular order.

For each sequence in the collection of sequences (set via the **live.step** object's *nseq* message), you'll see a list of each sequence in the stack as a series of lists – one list for each step of your sequence. The list consists of the number of the step, followed by the five values (pitch, velocity, duration, and the two "extra" values) associated with it.

If we'd had two sequences (*nseq 2*) stored in our **live.step** object, the output you see would be twice as long – one 16-line set of lists for each step in the sequence for each of the two sequences. This is a very simple example, of course – the **live.step** object supports 16 sequences with up to 64 steps each, and up to five parameters (pitch, velocity, duration, and two extra parameters you can use for whatever you want), so the output could be pretty large indeed.

But the good news is that the dump output just cycles through everything in a nice predictable order, with one line per step. What we need is a way to take that line-by-line output and use it to create a dictionary.

Although the Max **dict** object provides us with lots of options, what we need is simple: a dictionary where each sequence in the collection can be addressed, and where each "step" in the sequence contains the five parameters associated with it. That means I'll need to created a dictionary whose entries are nested one level deep:

(sequence 1 (step data))
(sequence 2 (step data))

.

.

.

(sequence 16 (step data))

A little quality time with the **dict** object's help file suggests that we can use the *replace* message to stash step data inside the list of sequences. I can also store the 5 parameters as an array, which will make things a lot easier. The message needs to be in this form:

replace <sequence number>::<sequence step> <list of parameters>

This allows us to create the nesting we'll need, and – with those double colons – it looks like a job for the **sprintf** object.

The **dictionary_loader** abstraction in the *01_livestep_dictionary* patch does the parsing. It looks like this on the inside:

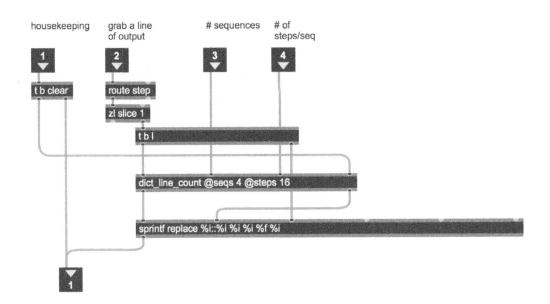

The **dictionary_loader** abstraction is what I'll use to pack the dump message's output into my dictionary. Here's what's going on in the patch:

- It clears the dictionary and handles count initializations

- The abstraction grabs a line of output from the **live.step** output and keeps count of which sequence and step we're grabbing

- It strips off the first bit of the list that the *dump* message sends out

- It constructs the *replace* message we need using a combination of **unpack** in addition to the **sprintf** object.

Here's what the inside of the **dict_line_count** abstraction looks like:

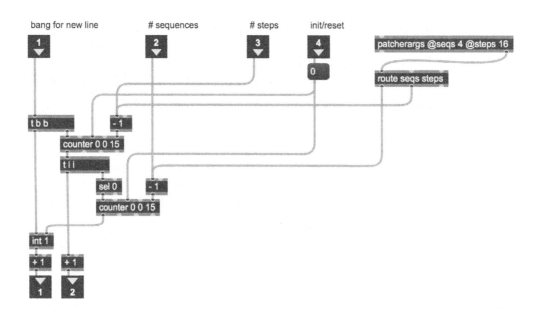

For this example, we're sticking with only 12 sequences of 12 steps each. But it would be nice to be able to use this same subpatcher in any situation, so the subpatch itself allows us to set an arbitrary number of sequences and steps. And I've also added a **patcherargs** object in order to allow the use of attributes (*@seqs* and *@steps*) to set the default values when I instantiate my object.

We're showing you these lower-level subpatchers as examples of the kinds of patching in Max/MSP that you'll be doing as your Maxing skills develop. As they improve, Max programmers move beyond the idea that there's a single object that performs any given task; they use their understanding of how Max processes information to create their own tools that not only fit a specific task, but which can be generalized to handle more than the problem before them at the moment.

We can now hook this all together and load up our dictionary with the data from the **live.step** object with a click of the mouse. Here's a piece of what our dictionary looks like:

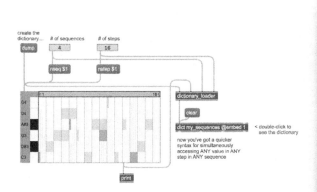

Note

One way to think of this patch is that we can now use the *live. step* object as a quick way to edit our sequence and then to store the new information to our dictionary – a judiciously placed *trigger* object would do that for us in a jiffy. I'll leave how to do it as an exercise for you...

Using The Dictionary

Now that we're working with dictionary data instead of the **live.step** data, we no longer need to specify targets to fetch information – it's a matter of using the *get* message.

The message *get 1::4* will fetch the five values for the fourth step of the first sequence and output a list consisting of the query followed by those values from the **dict** object's second outlet.

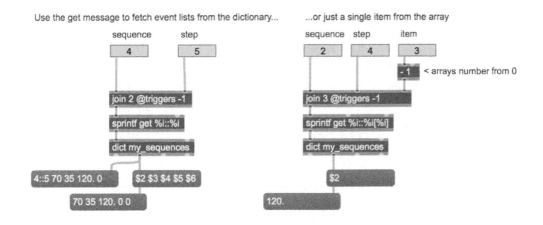

Similarly, the message *get 2::2[2]* will output the duration value (i.e. the third item in the 5-item list – remember, arrays number from zero!) for the second step of the second sequence only.

From Many Queries, One

These messages set up your "multiple choice" UI for outputs. There are a number of directions you can go from here. For example, you could use Cycling '74's M application as a model and create a step sequencer where each of your parameters is constructed using a separate **live.step** object whose only output is set to a group of possible note values.

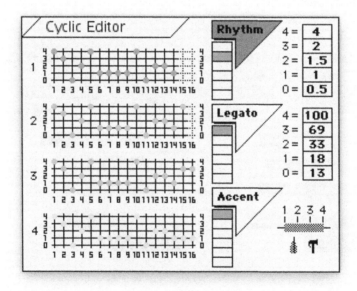

With this dictionary in play, you can now start creating events using the dictionary you've created to construct arbitrary sequencer events. I'll end this tutorial with a couple of examples of various possibilities.

Perhaps the simplest idea involves constructing hybrid sequences. You could create MIDI note messages by grabbing individual parts that make up the MIDI message from *entirely different sequences*. In addition, you could use different loops or subsets of the sequences to do so, and then combine them to produce a wealth of different sequences from a limited set of data.

The *02_livestep_dictionary_2* example patch provides an example of that technique at work. It grabs an up/down cycle of 11 from sequence 1 for the pitches, a loop between 2 and 10 from sequence 7 for velocities, and a regular cycle backwards through the durations in sequence 11 to produce its output:

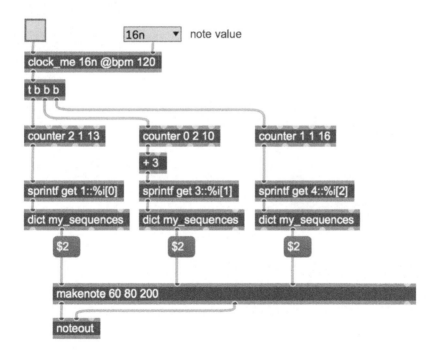

Sometimes the "shape" of the data itself gives you ideas of interesting things to try – the *03_livestep_dictionary_3* file is an example of that.

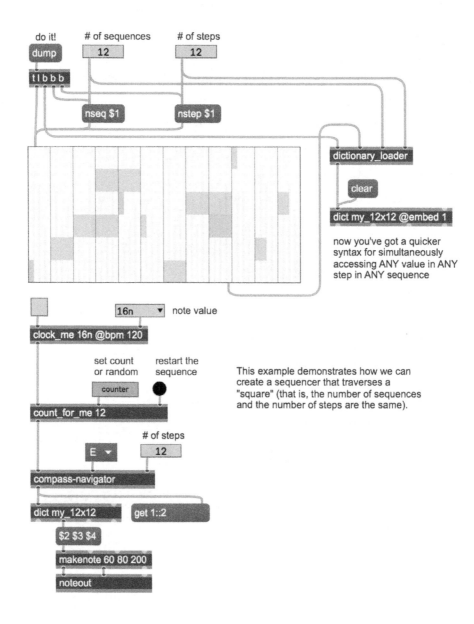

now you've got a quicker syntax for simultaneously accessing ANY value in ANY step in ANY sequence

This example demonstrates how we can create a sequencer that traverses a "square" (that is, the number of sequences and the number of steps are the same).

For this example, I'd originally started with a collection of twelve sequences of twelve steps each. I had 12-tone rows in mind, but realized that I had another interesting opportunity offered by the data structure – I could take a **counter** object and traverse my 12 x 12 set of sequences by stepping through each step in the sequence on one of the twelve sequences in the collection (which would give twelve MIDI note events) or I could step through a single step in each of the twelve separate sequences in the collection to produce my output. Once I started thinking of this traversal in terms of the idea of "north/south" (the stack) versus "east/west" (the sequence), I realized that I could also step through the data set in four more "directions" (northeast, southeast, and so on). It took a little while to patch, but I think it was totally worth it.

The work associated with traversing the collection of sequences in one of 8 directions is handled by the **compass_navigator** abstraction. Here's what's inside:

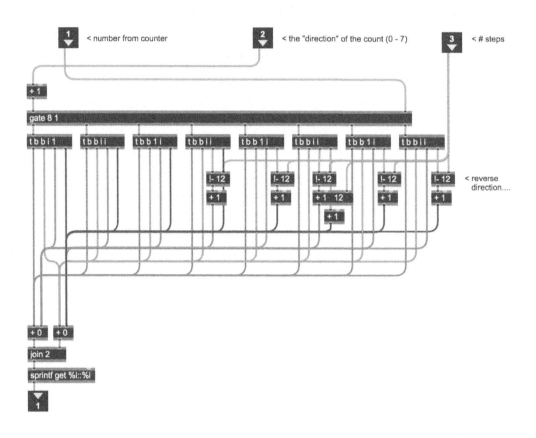

For each tick of the **clock_me** abstraction, the following operations occur:

- A number from the **count_for_me** abstraction is received.

- The abstraction uses the "compass direction" chosen to decide which portions of the *get* message need to be incremented or decremented.

- The abstraction collects and formats a 2-item list that will fetch the parameters from our dictionary used to construct the MIDI note message.

I'm sure there are a lot of interesting things you might try (loading the array with actual 12-tone rows, for example).

And – again – the advantage of driving our step sequencer using a count is that we can use all kinds of interesting and exotic counting techniques.

We've patiently gone step by step so far, and now... it's time to *swing*.

Learning To Swing

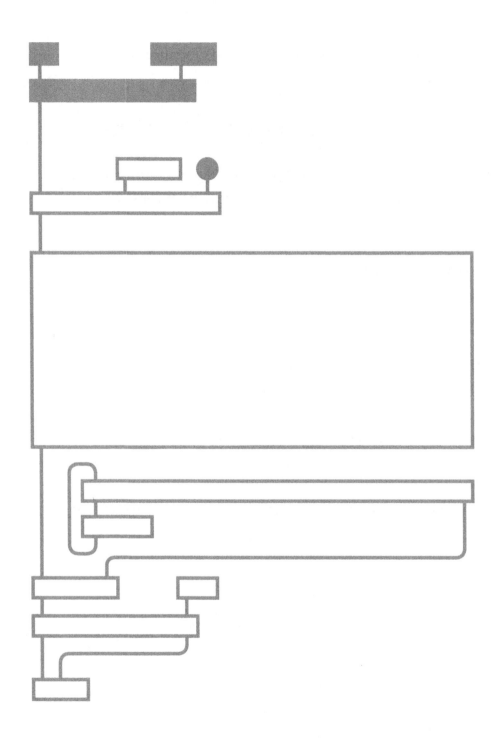

In all kinds of styles of popular music, notes will be played unevenly rather than using precise metronomic time. That unevenness tends to happen with pairs of notes, where the delay between the first and second note in the pair is *just a bit longer* than the second. The practice is commonly referred to as swing or shuffle.

Some people prefer to use the word 'shuffle' to describe this way of varying the timing in rhythm – the use of the word has an interesting history, especially when used by jazz critics or historians. It even has an interesting history on the Max Forum itself. While I'm aware of the arguments, the word 'swing' is in far more common use than 'shuffle' by most people, and I'll be using it here.

Scholars and researchers who have studied "swing" have found that the amount of those delays varies from one style of music to another, from one player to another, and even with the tempo of the music itself.

Since that's the case, I'm going to begin this chapter by doing some patching that takes tempo into account and calculating an amount of delay as a percentage of a note value – the patch will group notes in pairs and delay playing the second note in the pair. That will give us a simple place to start.

The *01_swing_shuffle* patch demonstrates this technique in action.

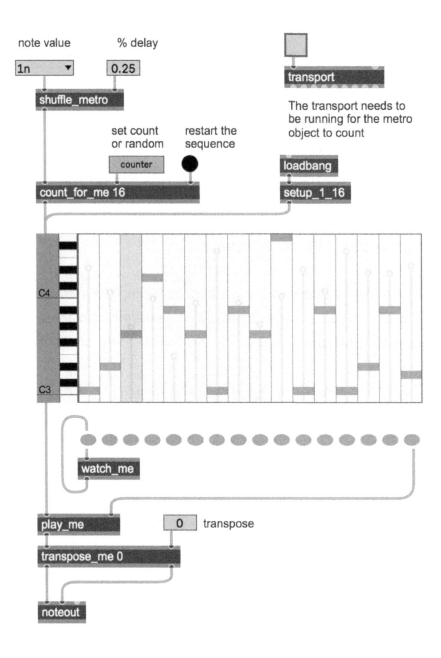

The only difference between this patch and our original simple step sequencer is a single patcher: the **shuffle_metro** abstraction.

Here's what's inside:

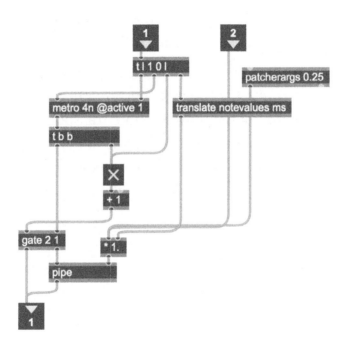

The basic patch is straight-ahead: *bang* messages from a **metro** object are grouped together in sets of two via some logic that uses a **toggle** object to transform the **metro** input into a sequence of zeros and ones, which is converted to ones and twos by a **+ 1** object that routes the *bang* message to separate outlets of a **gate** object for odd and even-numbered bang messages. The odd numbered (1) *bang* messages are passed through as they are, while each even-numbered (0) *bang* message is delayed by a fixed amount using the **pipe** object. The amount of the delay is set as a percentage value: 0% passes the second *bang* message through with no delay, 50% delays the even-numbered message by half the value of the **metro** object, and so on.

How did we figure out how many milliseconds to delay that second *bang* when we're using Max note values to set the **metro** object and we don't necessarily know the tempo? There's a Max object for that: the **translate** object. You can use arguments to set the kind of input you expect and the output you want, and the **translate** object does the conversion for you while keeping track of the tempo of your transport. In our patch, the **translate notevalues ms** object calculates the time between *bang* messages from the **metro** object, and then sets the amount of delay we use when calculating the percentage of shuffle to send to the delay.

Playing Early (and often)

The simple swing patch is a great and simple way to add variety to your sequences, but it doesn't necessarily *always* resemble the behavior of human musicians.

Here's how our simple patch is a tad too reductive: Sometimes, human musicians will play not only behind the beat (in terms of a metronome), but slightly *ahead* of a beat as well. We can't really use a simple delay patch to represent that very well.

In order to represent that, we'll need some different Max patching – a technique that gives us room to adjust our beats behind *or* ahead. The next two example patches provide us with two different methods to approach the problem, and that differ in some interesting ways.

The *02_shuffle_swing* patch maintains the idea that our beats come in pairs, with one beat being slightly behind the other, but it adds the ability to make the shift backwards, so that the first beat is slightly ahead of the second.

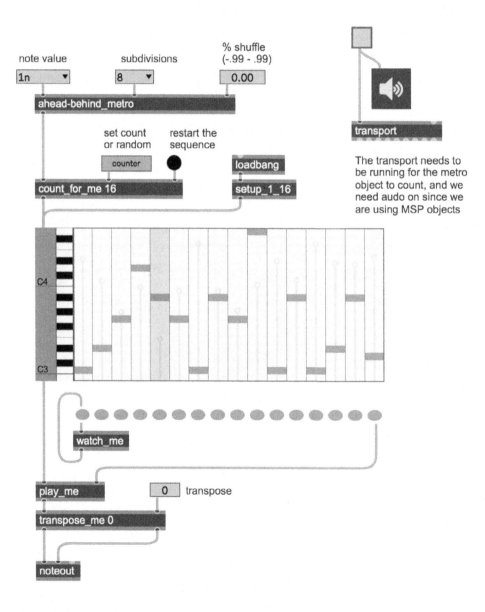

It's also a little different in two other ways:

1. It makes use of working with MSP signals at audio rate to handle the
   timing chores, and involves some interesting approaches to combining
   and folding signals.

2. It's a patch that's not selected because it was easy to understand. The
   patch we're about to see is a deep and subtle bit of MSP patching
   based on the work of Peter McCullough. While it might not be as easy
   to follow as some of the other patches you'll encounter in this book,
   spending some time with it and understanding how Peter solved the
   problem will be a great exercise.

The *shuffle_swing_2* patch replaces only one piece of our original simple
step sequencer – an abstraction called **ahead-behind_metro** that
replaces the original **clock_me** abstraction. The patcher lets you choose
an overall unit of time (as note values) and then subdivide that duration
into subdivisions of 4, 8, 16, or 32 units. By default, the amount of swing
is set to 0. As you increase that value in a positive direction, you'll get the
same effect as in the first example patch – the second beat in each pair
will be delayed by some amount (e.g. .33 is a triplet's worth of delay, .5 is
a delay of half the value of the beat, and so on). However, if you input a
negative number, the effect will be that the second note is played *earlier*
than expected. At the high and low ranges in both directions, both the
first beat and the second beat will be smashed together.

The **ahead-behind_metro** abstraction uses a technique for generating bang messages (similar to the **metro** object) – working with signals at audio rate, and then converting those signals to provide us with *bang* messages.

Let's take a look inside:

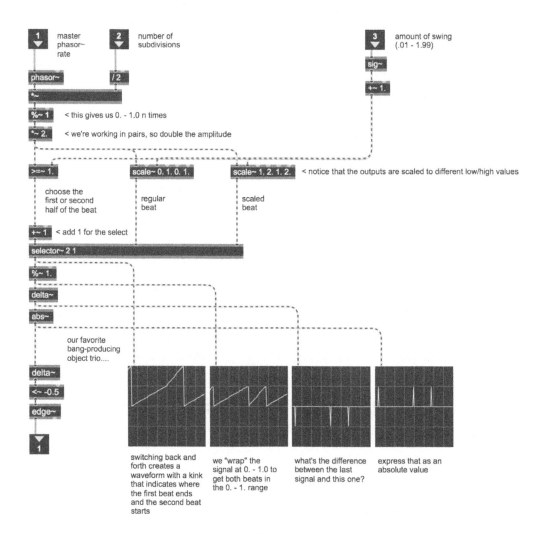

As with our n-tuplet metronome, we work with a single master **phasor~** object whose rate is set using note values. The middle inlet of the **ahead-behind_metro** abstraction takes a value that specifies how many subdivisions of our master **phasor~** we want, available with values of 4, 8, 16, or 32 subdivisions. Since this patch is also working with pairs of *bang* messages, we divide that value by half (since we need 4 pairs for 8 values, etc.).

Next, we perform an interesting trick you'll be seeing again – we multiply the **phasor~** object's output by the number of pairs and then use the **%~ 1**. object to "wrap" the output to give us a ramp signal that ramps the same number of times as we need to calculate our offset pairs.

So we have a signal that ramps from 0. - 1.0 at a rate that corresponds to the pair of *bang* messages.

Here's where Peter McCullough's solution gets interesting. He uses a floating-point message in the range of -.99 - .99 to generate a pair of separate ramp waveforms that are scaled in two different output ranges. One **scale~** object scales the input ramps by using the swing/shuffle value (-.99 - .99) as the high input range for an output in the range 0. - 1.0. The other **scale~** object takes the same swing/shuffle value and scales the input ramps by using the swing/shuffle value (-.99 - .99) as the low input range for an output in the range 1.0 - 2.0.

In addition, the swing/shuffle value is used to choose an output from the two newly scaled ramps by testing the swing/shuffle value using a **>=~** object. Doing that testing creates a really fast signal-rate switch. You'll notice that since the **>=~** object's output is a zero or one, we'll need to add one to the output to the **selector~** object (since an input of zero would close all the inputs).

The result of this operation is something really interesting: an output waveform in the range of 0. - 2.0 that will have a "kink" for any value other than 0. (which corresponds to no shuffle/swing at all). The skew in the output waveform indicates where the first beat ends and the second beat starts. The magic of this particular solution becomes apparent when we do something really simple – we use that **%~ 1**. object once again to constrain the waveform output to the 0. - 1.0 range. The elegant result is a pair of ramps that – as a pair – always takes the same amount of time regardless of whether the shorter section is first or second.

The task left to us now is to translate those ramps to *bang* messages. In this patch, we take the kinked and folded waveform and the MSP **delta~** object to keep track of the difference between the last signal value and the current one, which gives us a set of "drops" in the resulting output. The MSP **abs~** object gives us the absolute value of the signal, which results in a set of spikes. We can use our old friends the **delta~/<~ .5/ edge~** MSP object trio to generate the *bang* messages we use to drive our step sequencer.

Every bang for Itself

While the patch *02_shuffle_swing* freed us from the idea that we can only play behind the beat, it does maintain the idea that our beats always come in pairs. For the third and final example patch in this chapter, we'll do some patching that will let us work with a sequence of individual time units that we can adjust ahead of or behind the beat.

To achieve this, we'll need to rethink our patch a little bit. We'll need to think of the sequence of *bang* messages for our step sequencer as defaulting to the *middle* of a range instead of starting at the beginning and being offset afterward. This lets us choose a value to the left of center to "rush" our event, while values to the right of that center will function as before.

When you think of it, what we're starting to see is a very different kind of metronome – one whose output is a sequence of intervals of time that vary across the length of our sequence.

The *03_swing_shuffle* patch is an example of this technique. It's patched with the assumption that each beat is at the *midpoint* of a unit of time, and then adding or subtracting an offset value from each individual step independently.

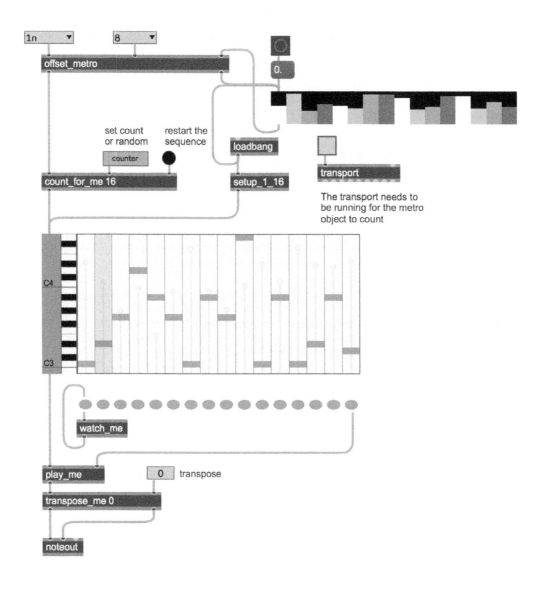

Let's look inside the **offset_metro** abstraction to see how we do it.

You'll see some familiar Max objects here, but the approach is slightly different. For one thing, we're setting the value of our **metro** object by using milliseconds rather than Time Value Syntax values directly. We're using the **translate** object to convert our base time value to milliseconds and then dividing it by the number of subdivisions we want to use. The number of subdivisions also sets the number of steps we use when counting through the list of offset values that we'll feed to the **delay** object for our output. We calculate the step offsets using the **zl lookup** object to grab the proper offset value from the input list and then add 0.5 to it to set the multiplier for calculating a delay offset.

Another Source of Enlightenment

While our final patch is interesting, it, too, isn't the only way to implement shuffle/swing in Max. If you're interested in pursuing this subject further, you might want to have a look at Darwin Grosse's elegant Javascript implementation of shuffle/swing contained in the BEAP Gate Sequencer module.

You'll find it by clicking on the **B** icon to the left of your patcher window, choosing the Sequencer tab from the menu, and clicking on and dragging the name Gate Sequencer into your unlocked patcher window. Since the Gate Sequencer module is a Max patch, you can open it up and examine Darwin's solution for yourself.

Next up – the end. The final destination, as far as our step sequencer is concerned: the output.

The Next Step(s)

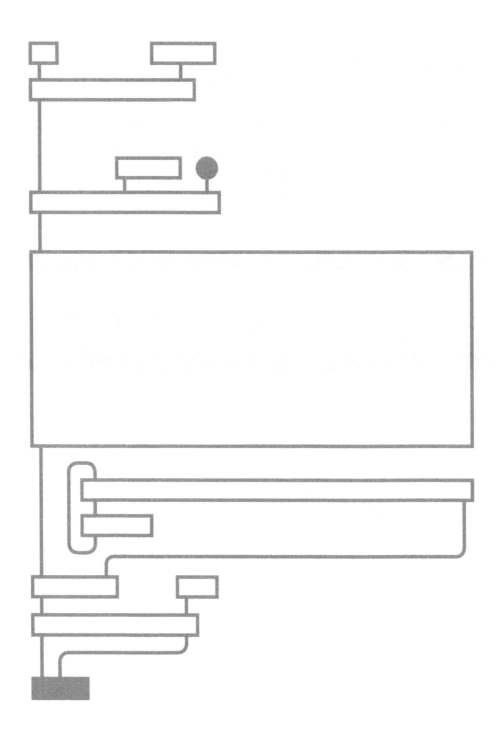

We've patiently made our way through almost every portion of our basic step sequencer patch, and looked at ways to generate and organize variety in the context of each of those pieces. Here we are at the last little box in our patch diagram – the end.

Or the beginning.

Throughout the chapters in this book, we've created a collection of variations on our basic step sequencer patch, which can serve as the starting point for your own work – combining the variants from one chapter with parts taken from another. For me, this final tutorial chapter is also an opportunity to meditate on that last little box – the Max **noteout** object – and to consider a few more possible futures based on the idea of *what* information you're sending and where you're sending the information *to*.

Thinking Beyond the Note

The **noteout** object in our simple sequencer patch really isn't the end of the line in our patch – rather, it transmits MIDI note-on and note-off messages. What's on the receiving end may vary – if you're working with Max/MSP, the destination could be a hardware synth, a software synth hosted by the MSP **vst~** or **amxd~** objects, or a channel on a DAW. If you're working with Max for Live, the destination for the **noteout** object will be a software synth or synth hosted on the Live channel where the device is located.

It's useful to remember that what your Max patch is really sending is *messages* – collections of numbers or lists or symbols mean something only when they are received elsewhere. In this chapter, we're going to think about what other messages we might send, and other places to send that information.

The great thing about Max is that it works with nothing *but* numbers and messages, and those can be used and/or modified to do all kinds of different things. So let's think about our step sequencer as a Max patch that outputs a bunch of messages in a general sense. What could we do with that?

If you're an analog synth person, I imagine you've already thought of one possibility – with every *bang* message from our clock, the **live.step** object outputs up to 5 separate messages that we've been working with all along – MIDI note number, velocity, duration, and the extra1 and extra2 messages. With the exception of the duration message, they're all values in the same range (0 – 127). Wouldn't it be great if we could use those outputs as control voltages for our analog rack?

The *CV_sequencer* example patch demonstrates how we can modify our simple step sequencer to create a sequencer that outputs control voltages to send to our analog equipment:

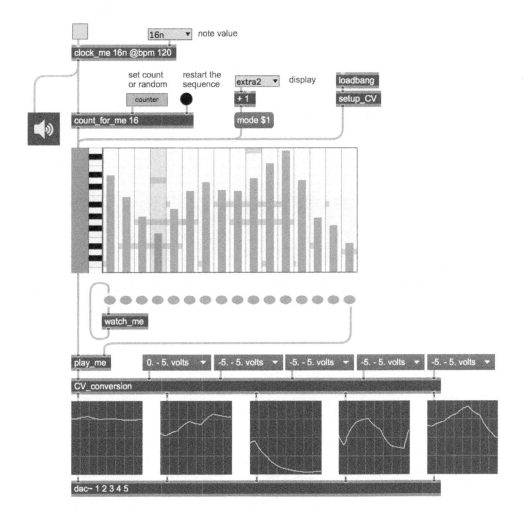

The changes to our main patch were fairly minimal, really. First, the **setup_CV** abstraction enables the output of the *extra1* and *extra2* parameters in addition to the setup we've usually done.

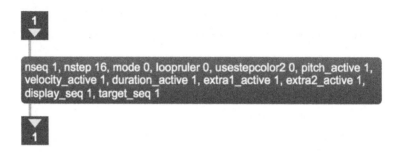

We also used the **live.menu** object's Inspector to add the two additional extra1 and extra2 menu items.

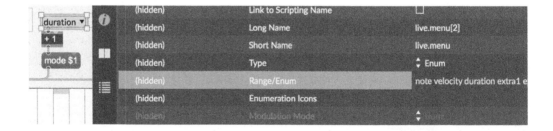

Numbers As Voltages

The rest of the work we've done in the patch can be found in the **CV_conversion** abstraction:

We need to make two modifications to our simple step sequencer:

- We need a way to convert our messages into voltages in the range our analog synth expects. Those ranges will vary depending on what kind of analog synths we're working with (for example, Eurorack systems work with three different voltage ranges: 0 to 1.0, 0. to 5.0, or -5.0 to +5.0 volts).

- We need to set up an interface that lets us send those output voltages to our synth.

Let's look at converting those values first. We'll start with the note number, velocity, and the two extra parameters first – since they're all just numbers in the range 0 - 127, all we need to do is to scale the input range to the output voltage range we need (in this example, I'll be working with a range of 0 – 5 volts). The perfect Max object for that is the **scale** object. The **scale** object lets you set a minimum and maximum input range, a minimum and maximum output range, and then it scales any input it receives to match the two ranges. When you're working in a situation where those ranges don't change, you can just use arguments to set the ranges (e.g. **scale 0 127 0. 5.**). Remember – if you want floating-point inputs or outputs, you'll need to add a decimal point to your arguments!

The only thing left to do is to convert those floating-point values to a signal that MSP objects can work with. The most common way to do that is to use the **sig~** object. It takes a number value as an input, and then outputs the current value once every time the MSP audio-rate scheduler "ticks," producing an output signal.

There's just one more little adjustment we might want to make – the *number_to_CV* example patch shows us the nature of the problem:

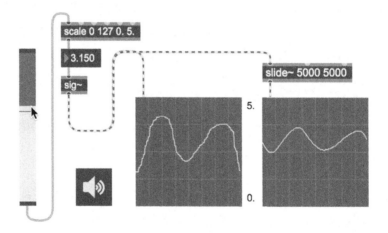

When we're sending numbers to the **scale** object at a high rate of speed or sending values that change by a considerable amount, we get jagged edges in the **sig~** object's output. That's because – as fast as we are – the sig~ object is making its conversions at a much faster rate. In order to produce a smoother output, we've added a **slide~ 5000 5000** object to the patch. The **slide~** object logarithmically filters its input to provide those smoother transitions between values over time.

Putting all those things together gives us the contents of an abstraction called **CV_conversion**:

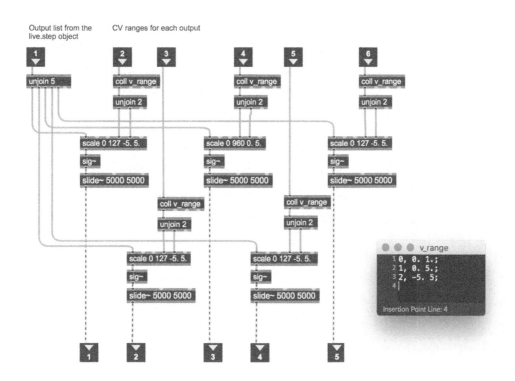

The abstraction is composed of five versions of our number-to-signal convertor. The left inlet unpacks the message from the **live.step** object and distributes each to a **scale** object (the duration values from inlet 4 are in a different range, so the arguments are different). The other **inlet** objects to the patch take output from a **umenu** item in the parent patch and use the output as an index to a list of output voltages stored in the **coll v_range** object (whose contents are shown in the *v_range window*). Finally, we convert the value to an MSP signal and smooth the result.

How do we get the output from the *CV_sequencer* abstraction to our analog gear? That will depend on your own output hardware. In my case, I'm using an audio interface that lets me send DC-coupled output voltages. If you have a module such the Expert Sleepers ES-8, you can use that, too. Instead of a **noteout** object, I've added a **dac~ 1 2 3 4 5** object to my patch, and connected each output from the **CV_conversion** abstraction to one of the inlets.

All I need to do to make use of my output voltages is to choose my interface in the Audio Status panel (found under the **Options** menu) in Max, use the display umenu in my patch to select which of the five output voltage curves I want to generate, click and drag, and turn on the patch.

Numbers As Parameters – VST/Audio Unit Plug-ins

Another possibility for re-purposing our step sequencer in Max involves using it with Instrument plug-ins hosted by the Max **vst~** object. We don't mean merely sending MIDI note events to a softsynth hosted in a **vst~** object – we talked about that in way back in Chapter 1. Instead, we want to think of our step sequencer as a source for parametric control of hosted plug-ins – the ability to have a step sequencer that twists the knobs on a VST or Audio Units plug-in.

The MSP **vst~** object not only lets us load and play VST or Audio Units MIDI instrument plug-ins and use their output in our patching, but we can also send Max messages that will let us modify the plug-ins *themselves*.

The **vst~** object's help file shows us what those messages look like:

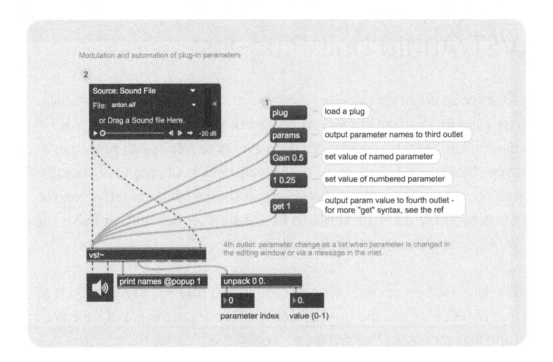

There are some useful messages shown here: We can use the *params* message to request a list of all of the parameters in a loaded plug-in, and – once we know the name or the number of the parameter, we can send it a name or number followed by a floating-point value in the range of 0. to 1.0 to set the parameter. That's very useful.

But how can we send those messages and then collect the parameter output in a way that we can easily use? The *VST_hosting_parameters* example patch provides a simple example of the kind of patching we can use to set that up.

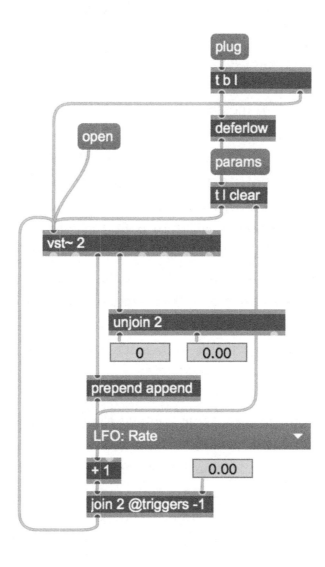

This patch will let you load a plug-in by clicking on the **message** box reading *plug* at the very top. It sends that message to the **vst~** object, and then sends a bang message to a **deferlow** object. The **deferlow** object is used to de-prioritize any Max message it receives—it puts all incoming messages at the tail of the low priority queue. We're using it here as a kind of "smart delay" to make sure that the **vst~** object is finished loading whatever plug-in we tell it to load (using the *plug* message) before we send a *bang* message to the **message** box object containing the *params* message.

After the plug-in is loaded, the patch uses a **trigger** object to control the order of operations. It sends a *clear* message to the **umenu** object that we'll use to store the parameter names, and then sends a *params* message to the **vst~** object, which responds by sending a complete list of its parameters in numerical order out the **vst~** object's second outlet. The patch uses a Max **umenu** object to collect the list of parameters – sending the parameter name messages to a **prepend append** object will precede each parameter name's output by the message *append*, which the **umenu** object understands to be a command to add it to its menu item list.

The result is a **umenu** object that contains all of the names of all of the parameters for any VST or Audio Units plug-in we've loaded. Altering a parameter is done by choosing its name from the **umenu** object and formatting a message that has that item's index number as its first item and a floating-point value between 0. and 1.0 as the second item in the list – in this example patch, we're using the all-hot-inlet version of the **join** object (**join 2 @triggers -1**) to do that.

Just in case you'd like to verify what you're doing, the patch includes a few extra messages. The *open* message will display the "front panel" of any VST/Audio Units plug-in you're hosting. In case you're not sure of what the number for any parameter on a plug-ins front panel is, you can always twist the knob or the move slider or press the button and then watch the list of two items output by the **unjoin 2** object connected to the **vst~** object's fourth outlet.

The *02_plug-in_sequencer_patch* takes this patching, and combines it with patching we've already done to allow us to sequence parameter values for VST/Audio Units plug-ins:

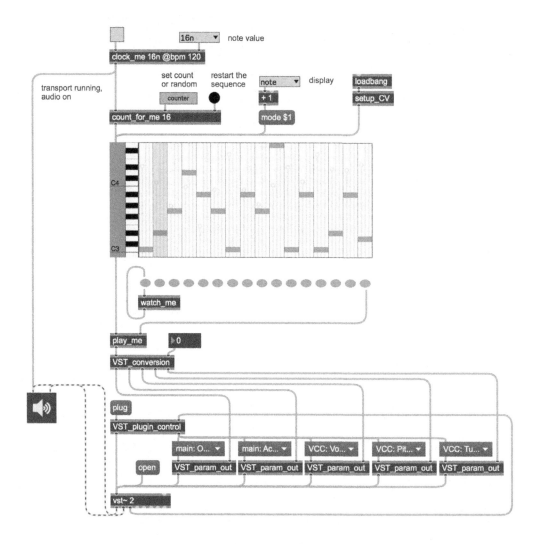

We're used the *CV_sequencer_patch* as the starting point for this patch, along with the the patching we just discussed. Max programmers reuse their old patches all the time, adding the new bits necessary for the new task. In this case, we already have quite a lot of what we need in terms of massaging the **live.step** object's output from our previous patching – the **CV_conversion** abstraction already offered us the possibility to scale sequencer output to a range of 0. - 1.0, so we can simplify the **CV_conversion** abstraction by removing all of the other scaling logic. In addition, out VST/Audio Units plug-ins aren't expecting their messages to be sent at signal rate – normal message rate will do perfectly well.

If our step sequencer's **clock_me** abstraction is running at slower clock rate (*1n* or *1nd*, for example) it would be useful to have the ability to smooth output data over longer lengths of time between outputs from the
live.step object – so let's convert those signal values back to message-rate using the **snapshot~ 20**. object, which samples audio-rate output at a predetermined rate. In addition, let's add a way to change the rate of data smoothing, too.

The result of our simplified **CV_conversion** abstraction patching – now renamed **VST_conversion** looks like this:

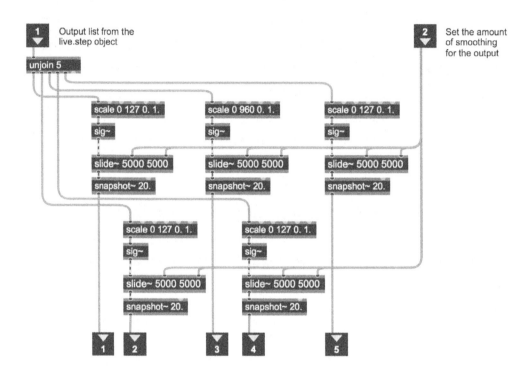

The **VST_plug-in_control** abstraction takes the contents of our earlier proof-of-concept *VST_hosting_parameters* patch and rearranges the inlets and outlets to be a little more manageable:

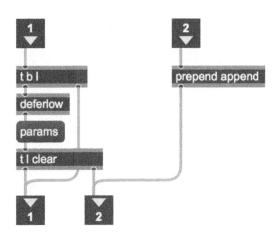

The result gives us a patch that lets us load a VST/Audio Units plug-in by clicking on the **message** box labeled plug, choose a group of parameters we want to modify from the **umenu** objects, and set the rate at which those outputs will be smoothed. Presto – plug-in parameter control!

Numbers As Parameters – AMXD Devices

Max 7 added the ability to host Max for Live MIDI Instrument devices using the **amxd~** object. In Chapter 1, we described how to modify the *01_simple_step_sequencer* patch to use the **amxd~** object as a destination for our step sequencer output. In addition, the **amxd~** object also gives us access to the parameters of any Max for Live instrument hosted by the device.

As was the case with the **vst~** object, re-purposing step sequencer outputs for use to control those parameters involves two tasks:

1. Formatting the output into messatges we can send to the **amxd~** object to change those parameters.

2. Scaling the output data from the **live.step** object to the parameter data range that the **amxd~** object expects to work with.

Handling the first task is going to require a little extra work as compared to working with VST and Audio Units plug-ins. The **amxd~** object uses a different way to address parameters (it does so *only* by parameter name), and we don't automatically know what the range of any parameter in a Max for Live instrument is in advance – we'll need to ask the hosted instrument about each parameter in turn and then store the range of values when we load the instrument.

Let's start by looking at how we can get a list of the parameters associated with an instrument we load.

A look at the Automation tab for the **amxd~** object's help file shows us that we can send a message to the object in the form *<parameter name> <number>* to set a parameter, but not how we find out what the parameters are or their range (minimum and maximum values), however.

If we look down the listing of attributes and messages for the object in the right-hand listing of the **amxd~** object's help file, there's something useful looking – a message called *getparams*.

Clicking on the message displays a helpful description at the bottom of
the listing:

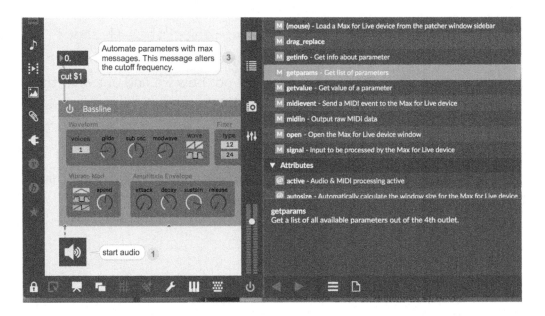

Since the help file is a Max patch, I can investigate this message a little
by unlocking the help patch, adding a **message** box containing the
getparams message, and then attaching a Max **print** object to the right
outlet of the **amxd~** device.

When I do that, lock the patch, and then click on the *getparams* **message** box, here's what I see in the Max console:

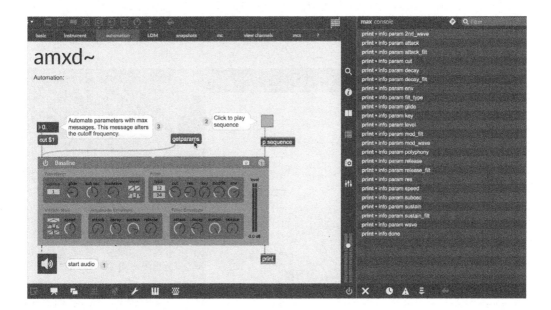

There's also a message listed right above the *getparams* message – the *getinfo* message. Adding another **message** box and sending the message *getinfo <parameter name>* (in this case, for the cut parameter) gives me this output in the console:

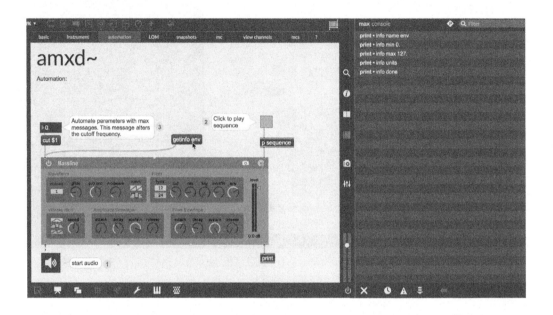

Note:

When I'm finished with these investigations, I close the help patch without saving to keep it neat and clean.

Here's what we need to do to set up using our step sequencer program to modify Max for Live instrument parameters:

1. We need to send a *getparams* message when we load any new instrument, which will output a list of all of an instrument's parameters.

2. For each of those parameters, we need to send a *getinfo* message and the grab the min and max values for the parameter.

3. We need to collect the parameter name and the parameter range and store them for later use.

All this work is done using the **AMXD_parameters** abstraction. Here's the inside of the abstraction that takes care of all that – it's worth a little serious study, given the complexity of what it does:

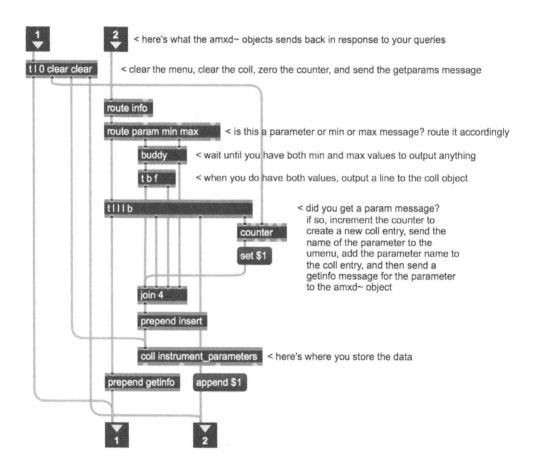

The easiest way to store the data we need will be to use a Max **coll** object, which we've seen in use in previous chapters. This time, we're going to create the contents of the **coll** object on the fly as we load a new Max for Live instrument. The object we create will contain a numbered line for each parameter associated with the currently loaded Max for Live instrument, and will take the form

<line number> <parameter name> <min value> <max value>

Performing these three tasks involves a little housekeeping: Every time we ask about the parameters for an instrument, we need to clear the UI objects of their current contents, empty out the **coll** object that's storing the parameter information we're interested in, and reset the **counter** object that keeps track of the number of parameters. This is the place where the Max **trigger** object really shines – it allows us to do the housekeeping any time we send that very first *getparams* message that starts things off, and to take the information that comes back from the **amxd~** or the **route** objects that separate out messages about parameter names from messages about min and max values.

We're going to need to make a few changes to the abstraction we created to use for VST parameters – since we need to know what the range for any given parameter is, the abstraction needs to be different for AMXD devices. The **coll instrument_parameters** object stores that information for us now, and we can make use of a nice feature of Max: global data spaces.

Anytime we create and fill a **coll** object and give it a name, we share those contents with any other coll object that has the same name anywhere else in our patch. The **AMXDparam_out** abstraction contains an example of that in action.

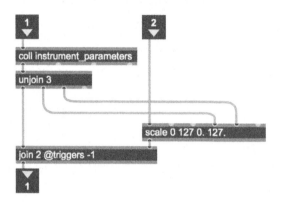

The left inlet takes a number that is the output of a **umenu** item in the parent patch and uses that as an index to a **coll instrument_parameters** object – the same name as the one that we created inside of the **AMXD_parameters** abstraction. Since the **coll** object has the exact same name, using it in this abstraction will give us the same results as we'd get from inside the **AMXD_parameters** abstraction. The patch takes the output list from the **coll** object (parameter name, min range, and max range), unpacks it, scales the input to the range for the AMXD parameter, and then sends out a list that has the name of the parameter followed by the properly scaled output value.

There's one final detail we'll need to attend to – the output from the duration part of the **live.step** object's list. Handling it is going to be a little different because we can't just automatically assume that the output scaling is going to be same.

Our patch contains a minor variation on the **VST_conversion** abstraction we used last time (we've renamed the abstraction **AMXD_conversion**):

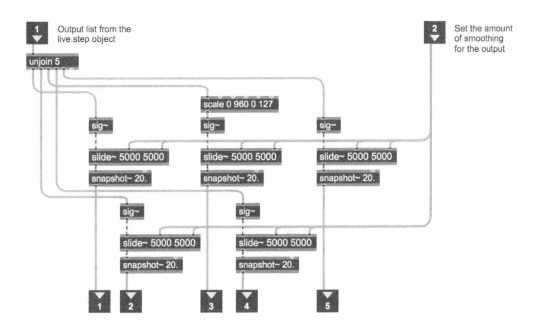

The changes are relatively minor. We've removed all but one of the **scale** objects, since we'll need to know the range for scaling and deal with that in another part of our patch. The only remaining scale object (**scale 0 960 0 127**) is used for the duration output – we're going to scale it so that its output is in the same range as all of the other inlets.

You can see the final result of all this patching in the *AMXD_hosting_parameters* patch, which includes an example of hosting the Max for Live MIDI instrument Big Ben Bell:

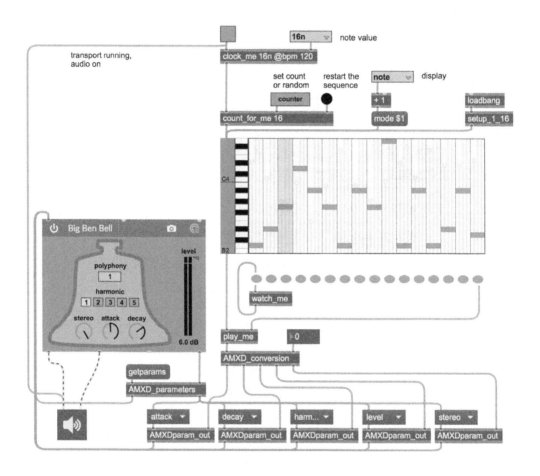

Numbers As Parameters – The Live Object Model

There's one other area where we can think about step sequencers as providing output as parameters rather than MIDI notes – something of particular interest to Max for Live users.

Max for Live allows users to access parts of the Live application itself. That means that we can take output from our step sequencer and use that to control aspects of the Live application that are available to us by using the Live Object Model. Let's begin by asking what the Live Object Model does and how does it interacts with Max.

You can access, observe, and control the Live application with Max patches by using a trio of Max objects : **live.object**, **live.path**, and **live. observer**. Working with the Live API in your Max for Live device involves using these objects to create a map of all of the parameters in your Live session, setting up communications with those parameters, and sending messages to control them.

There's a world of example programs in Max for Live that will introduce you to interesting things you can do using the Live Object Model. For the final part of this chapter, we're going to look at one of them – a piece of Max patching that will give you easy access to any part of your Live session file that's accessible via the Live Object Model.

For the second time in this book, we're going to use a piece of Max patching that someone else besides myself created – a piece of Max patching created by Manuel Poletti, who creates wonderful things for Max users and works at IRCAM in Paris.

One day, as I was looking through a set of Live tutorials about how to use Max to control Live devices, I came upon a Max for Live device in the tutorial session called *Max API ADial*, which lets you set up a connection to anything in a Live session and control it by using a **live.dial** object. Here's what the Max patch looked like once I opened the Max for Live device to edit it and turned off the Presentation Mode:

ADial Controlling a parameter in a Live device using the Live API

This device shows you how to use the live.remote~ object to control a single parameter of a device such as the gain of a filter in the EQ Eight device or the volume of a track in the Mixer device. A Max abstraction containing three popup menus let you browse the Live set and select a parameter. When you choose a parameter, the abstraction outputs the "ID" of that parameter and sends it to the live.remote~ object. The parameter will then be controlled solely by signal values received by the live.remote~ object (the parameter is grayed out in Live to indicate this). While control values in this patch are in the generic [0. 1.] range, this patch shows the real value of the controlled parameter, along with its min and max values. Turning off the Target sends an <id 0> message to the live.remote~ object, allowing the parameter to be accessed with the mouse or by other live.remote~ objects in other devices again.

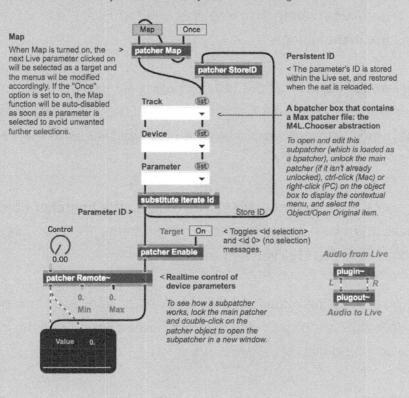

Map

When Map is turned on, the next Live parameter clicked on will be selected as a target and the menus wil be modified accordingly. If the "Once" option is set to on, the Map function will be auto-disabled as soon as a parameter is selected to avoid unwanted further selections.

Persistent ID

< The parameter's ID is stored within the Live set, and restored when the set is reloaded.

A bpatcher box that contains a Max patcher file: the M4L.Chooser abstraction

To open and edit this subpatcher (which is loaded as a bpatcher), unlock the main patcher (if it isn't already unlocked), ctrl-click (Mac) or right-click (PC) on the object box to display the contextual menu, and select the Object/Open Original item.

< Toggles <id selection> and <id 0> (no selection) messages.

< Realtime control of device parameters

To see how a subpatcher works, lock the main patcher and double-click on the patcher object to open the subpatcher in a new window.

This patch contained everything I needed to control the Live Object Model using Max. Even though the patch was daunting to open up and investigate, I figured out a couple of things right away:

- When I clicked on the "On" button, the patch generated a listing of every single parameter on every single device on every single track in my Live session, ready for me to choose what I wanted to control by using **live.menu** objects.

- The **live.dial** object that did the controlling did nothing more than to send floating-point numbers in the range of 0. - 1.0, which meant that I could use *anything* in Max that produced values in that range to control my Live session.

In your spare time, you should feel free to open the **bpatcher** objects that make up this patch and examine their contents. If you know very little about Max, I can tell you two things:

1. It is an astoundingly beautiful bit of Max patching - one of my personal models of a style of patching to which I aspire. If you're a beginner, it's also a bit daunting to figure out.

2. It might be more complex than the usual patches you look at, but, you don't need to know how it works in order to use it - you can drop it into your Max for Live devices, and - in the words of Steve Jobs - "It just works."

I copied the parts of the Max for Live device that did what I needed and saved the result for my own use – I created a Max file called LiveAPI-control and saved it as a Max snippet. I've been using it ever since. Here's what my snippet looks like (you'll find a copy of *LiveAPI-control.maxsnip* in the patches folder for this chapter):

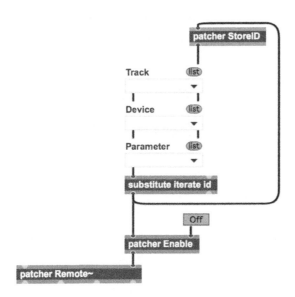

When creating a Max for Live device based on step sequencers such as those we've created in this book, all we need to do is to add one copy of this bit of patching for each parameter we want to use as a control for the Live application, and connect it to whatever outputs we want to use.

When viewed in Presentation mode, this bit of Max patching displays a nice, clean set of **live.menu** objects with control switches, together with an On/Off switch, ready to control a Live application parameter.

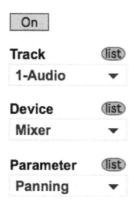

The examples folder for this chapter contains a Max for Live device that combines a version of our step sequencer patch together with a couple of these pieces of patching to create a step sequencer whose outputs can be used to control your Live session. Here's what the basic patch looks like:

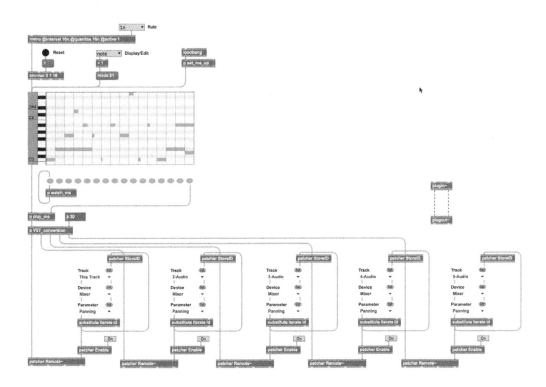

No surprises here. In fact, we borrowed the **VST_conversion** abstraction from the VST parameter sequencer as it was. Since it worked with a 0. to 1.0 data output range, it was all ready to go.

All we did was to add 5 copies of the LiveAPI-control patcher and connect its inlets to the outlets of the **VST_conversion** abstraction outputs, then save and close the device.

In practice using the Max for Live device is a breeze:

- Add a copy of the *M4L_parameter_sequencer* AMXD device to your patch.

- For each of the 5 outputs, click on the list buttons for the Track, Device, and Parameter menus.

- For each output click on the three menus to select a destination for your output.

- Click on the "On" button for each output, and off you go.

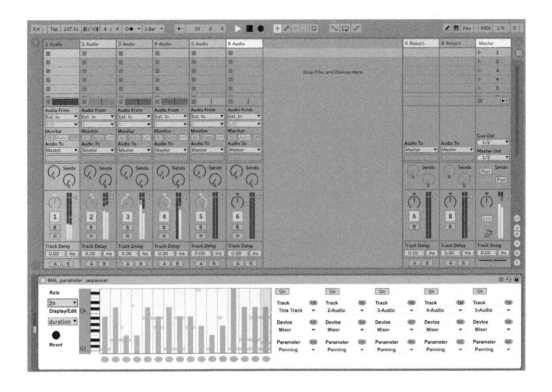

The next chapter isn't about new tricks – it's about what you've already done, and what you can do *next*.

Afterwords

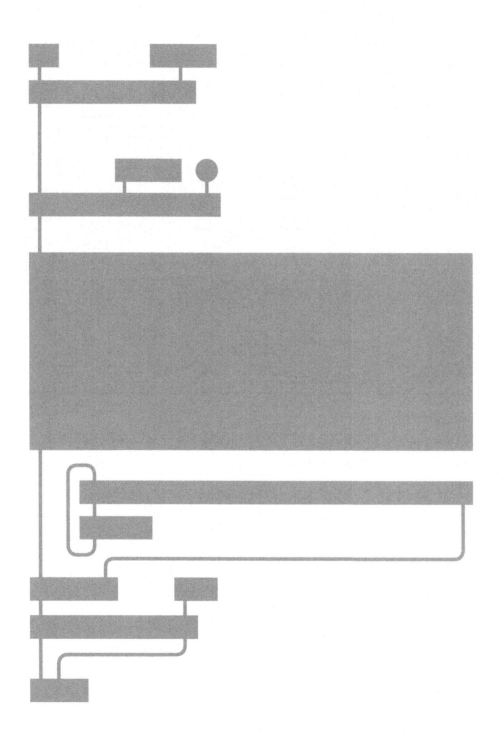

Here we are at the end, or – more likely – at *your* beginning. I'm glad you made it, and am grateful for your patience and attention. I'd like to say a few things before you go, if I may.

Big Ideas and Little Steps

As I said in the very beginning, the goal of this book wasn't to make the ultimate step sequencer patch. In a way, *you* are the best judge of something like that – we all have our own ideas of the form that the ultimate patch would take.

Instead, I've tried to take on what seems like a large idea in terms of Max patching, and show you how the idea can be broken up into smaller pieces that work together as a step sequencer.

As you continue to work, I expect that you'll be doing that a lot. Learning to take your big idea and to break it down into smaller and more manageable pieces is an important skill to learn and a useful habit of thought to develop.

Recombining and Making Hybrids

Instead of working toward a total and finished end product, I've also tried to take one piece of the big idea and to "build it out" – to start with a simple idea, to do some patching that adds or changes the way that an individual piece works. In a few places, I've even talked about taking a piece of patching I developed and using it in an entirely different part of the patch, or changing the order in which it was used. Max is about connecting things together, and it can be inspiring to change the order in which things are connected one to another.

Once you have the pieces, you can recombine them – you can go through each of the chapters and grab something that interests you in each piece, and then roll them all together to make something new, too. You can, in turn, also take those pieces and modify them to make your own pieces.

The Zen of All Max Patching (The Three Questions)

Whenever Max programmers patch, three questions are always at the heart of their next step.

This is not a deep, dark secret, but it is something that beginning Max users don't always consider when approaching a new problem. In my experience, it's something that people who work with Max regularly do all of the time, whether they think about it or not – it's something they think *with* rather than thinking about, perhaps.

Learning to program in Max is really all about learning a few simple basic ideas and a few go-to Max objects, and working with them to achieve your goal. If you can't solve the problem in front of you using them, it may be time to find a new object or a new technique. It's all about learning as you go.

Here are the three questions:

1. What kind of information does the last object in my current patching chain require in order to achieve my goal?

2. What kinds of input is my patch currently getting, and where does that input come from?

3. How can I connect or combine or create the input(s) to turn them into the kind of message(s) the *last* object in my patch is expecting in order to do its work?

And, once you've used those three questions to solve your problem, you repeat that same process to achieve your *next* goal. I hope that the patching I've done throughout this book has shown you that way of approaching such problems in real-life situations.

There are a lot of different Max objects out there. Since there are so many Max objects, people sometimes imagine that there must be a single Max object somewhere that will perform any given task. It's much more often the case that accomplishing a task involves adding a couple of Max objects rather than requiring a whole new object.

Recycling Your Best Ideas

When we patch with Max, we usually have a single problem in mind that we want to solve. But it's often the case that once we've solved a problem, we might find ourselves wanting to perform a similar task somewhere else that varies only slightly from our initial solution to that single problem. The savvy Max programmer is always on the lookout for those bits of patching, and always asking, "Is this something I could use again if abstraction was just a little bit more general?"

Often, it's the case that you'll make a patch that works with a specific number of items or a specific kind of input. When you get it working, ask yourself if you could change things just a little bit and have your patch be something you can use again, and use in different situations.

And when you do, here are two great ways to reuse your patch:

1. You can save the patch as an abstraction, as we've done all throughout this book. All you need to do to reuse it is to make sure it is in the same folder as the patch you're working on, or in your Max search path.

2. You can save your patch as a Max snippet, which lets you drag and drop if right into your patch. For more information on Snippets, type the word snippet into the search box in the upper right-hand corner of any patcher window and hit return. Max's Documentation Browser will open up and show you all kinds of resources related to your query. Click on Guides in the left-hand part of the Documentation Browser, and you'll find out more about them (In fact, using the Documentation Browser while patching is another good Max habit to cultivate).

And Finally, a Few Words of Thanks and Praise...

This book and the patching contained in it has benefited greatly from a number of my friends and colleagues, and I would like to thank them here.

Tim Place and Les Stuck were early and enthusiastic readers.

I'm grateful to Peter McCullough, Manuel Poletti, and Emmanuel Jourdan for their wonderful and instructive patching examples, and for their permission to include them here.

My writing always emerges from a careful and thoughtful editorial pass by my friend Darwin Grosse better than it was when he first received it – and that's true again.

To David Zicarelli and all of my colleagues at Cycling '74, I'd like to simply say, "Thanks for everything."

That's all I wanted to say. I hope this has been helpful to you.

Patch on, do good work, and keep in touch.

Gregory Taylor (gregory@cycling74.com)

Made in the USA
Las Vegas, NV
13 February 2022

43889778R00151